Longevity Solution

Compelling proof that royal jelly has the power to eliminate fatigue, provide greater energy and extend life

Dr. Cass Ingram

Knowledge House
Buffalo Grove, Illinois

Table of Contents

Dedication: To my dearest, who makes my life royal.

Acknowledgements: Credit is in the name of the most merciful God, the Maker. It is His blessed gift to us. My prayers are to all my readers, hoping for dthe best of health.

Introduction

To strive to be as healthy as possible is an ideal goal. Health is defined as a state of comfort, where the body functions at an optimal level, physically and mentally. Disease is defined as a state of distress. It is a disturbance, where the body is plagued with discomfort, pain, and disablement.

Modern medicine regards disease as incurable. Often, the proposed cure causes more damage than the disease itself. This has not always been the case. In ancient times numerous conditions were regarded as curable, plus the cure was natural and relatively non-toxic. The goal was always to cure disease. The fact is the ancients developed extensive experience with natural substances known to cure disease. Royal jelly was one of these substances.

God almighty inspired humankind to understand the potency of beehive products. The holy books, particularly the Qur'an and Bible, contain numerous references—and reverences—regarding them. The Qur'an glorifies the bee as one of God's finest creations, indicating that this creature works for the benefit of humankind. Obviously, the importance of the productions of these creatures is far greater than is commonly realized. The point is the original inspiration for the medicinal powers of honey came from God himself.

Ancient records reveal that royal jelly was used by the early Egyptians, but, certainly, numerous other earlier civilizations used it. It was one of Cleopatra's beauty secrets. Royal jelly may have been one of the vitality factors accounting for the strength and beauty of Egyptian royalty, including the Pharaoh's. The ancient Greeks consumed it to increase physical strength. Oriental rulers claimed that royal jelly helped them live longer and remain sexually potent even in old age.

Ancient uses are of value, because they provide information about potential cures. Many of today's most popular drugs were once used by various now defunct civilizations. In contrast to the environment today the ancients had no vested interest. Medical monopolies didn't exist. If a substance worked, they used it. They were free to explore the use of natural compounds, like royal jelly, for a wide range of illnesses. Thus, they discovered valuable uses for natural compounds that even today's scientists have failed to discern. Imagine the power of combining the wisdom of the ancients with the sophistication of modern science. With royal jelly, that power is available. In addition to the knowledge of past civilizations there exist modern scientific studies proving that royal jelly is a curative substance. Plus, there are hundreds of case histories of individuals who have benefited greatly and in some instances have been cured through its powers.

Vital substance

Royal jelly is a source of dense nutrition. Because it is nutrient dense, it is reserved by the bees only for their queens. The entire hive is dependent upon the queen; she lays up to 2,000 eggs daily, a monumental task for such a tiny creature. Thus, she must receive intensive nutritional support: amino acids, fatty acids, steroids, hormones, vitamins, and minerals, all of which are provided by royal jelly. The queen lives up to six years, while a worker bee lives six weeks. This means that the queen lives over 35 times longer than her workers. Both the queen and the workers, which are also females, begin as identical bee eggs. Royal jelly is the only thing which makes the difference. It induces a metamorphosis. What's more, it is exclusively royal jelly that is responsible for the queen's unique physiology, long life, physical power, and immense fertility.

It seems incredible that this nutritionally rich substance can actually convert a simple worker bee into a queen. Obviously, it is a magic elixir. No other substance is capable of such a phenomenal biological transformation.

For humans, taking royal jelly is a positive experience. If you take it regularly, expect to be transformed.

Only royal jelly can transform a worker into a queen. Numerous attempts have been made to synthesize it. The synthetic product, when fed to the bees, produces no results; the bees usually die. Only bees can correctly compose it. Humans will never be able to duplicate it.

Royal jelly is synthesized by bees and, like honey, is completely edible. In fact, all of the productions of bees are edible: propolis, royal jelly, bee pollen, and honey. Even the wax is partially digestible. Bee products have been used as food, as well as medicine, for thousands of years. They can be consumed in large quantities safely and with numerous benefits. Modern humanity has yet to utilize these products to their optimal potential. Royal jelly is perhaps the least utilized of all of these products.

Some authors have described royal jelly as "mysterious" or as a "gift fit for royalty" or the "elite." There is nothing mysterious about royal jelly. The fact is it is one of the most nutrient dense substances known. It is completely pure and nutritious, and this is what largely accounts for its medicinal powers. Royal jelly contains virtually everything the body needs for optimal health as well as for combating disease. Rather than induce some sort of unexplainable miracle, royal jelly aggressively nourishes cells, helping them to rebuild themselves. Few if any other foods meet this description.

The apparently mysterious actions of royal jelly are readily explained by its ingredients. For instance, it is one of the few hormone-rich foods. The hormones it contains are completely safe to ingest. Hormones are known to exert profound actions on human cells. It is listed as the richest source of certain vitamins, notably pantothenic acid, riboflavin, and biotin. It is an excellent source of amino acids, far superior to milk or eggs. Royal jelly is the only significant source of acetylcholine, an important neurotransmitter. Acetylcholine is needed for the transmission of nerve impulses throughout the brain and spinal cord. It contains other rare substances, like immunoglobulins, which are found in no other foods. A rare type of structural protein, a collagen-like substance, is also found in it. The latter is thought to account for its beautifying powers. The fact is no other substance matches its density of cellular and body-building components. This is why it can prove valuable for virtually everyone, because there is no such thing as perfect health. A universal tonic, like royal jelly, is likely to produce universal results, that is health improvement in virtually anyone who tries it.

Royal jelly is the broad-spectrum tonic that everyone desires. It is the only tonic proven by scientific studies to rejuvenate the body naturally and safely: hormones, neurotransmitters, enzymes, amino acids, immunoglobulins, hydroxy acids, collagen precursors, B vitamins, fat soluble vitamins, and minerals.

Recently, growth hormone has been touted as a longevity tonic, but it has never been proven safe. Royal jelly is the 100%

safe source of natural, rejuvenating hormones. It has everything the human body needs to rebuild, revive, regenerate, and survive. That is why it is perhaps the most vital and valuable substance known.

Powers of the hive

Bees are among the most industrious of all creatures. They spend their entire lives collecting plant compounds, many of which are, in essence, potent medicines. Plants are the original source of many of today's most popular medicines. Examples include aspirin, digitalis, penicillin, Taxol, and Nystatin. Bees make plant concentrates. Thus, they produce concentrated medicines. These natural medicines include honey, bee pollen, propolis, bee venom, and, of course, royal jelly. All of the bee productions provide significant medicinal properties, a fact which is easily proven both in human and test tube studies.

Regenerative factor

Rather than thinking of royal jelly as a magic elixir or fountain of youth, let us look at its value from a physiological viewpoint. Every day the human body undergoes a variety of processes which are essential to its existence. Cells die and are born. They become diseased or cured. They regenerate or decay. The body is constantly attempting to rebuild itself, to avoid the onset of disease, toxicity, and decay. Yet, it needs a wide range of nutritive substances to do so. This is why royal jelly is so vital. With its immense nutritional and biochemical profile, it aids in the natural regenerative processes by supplying precisely what the body needs. Thus, it helps the cells heal themselves.

Aging is clearly associated with a decline in cellular nutrition. When the cells become deficient in nutrients, they age rapidly. If they are well supplied with all of the nutrients they need, they remain vital. Aging is also associated with a decline in hormone levels. In fact, one of the signs of premature aging is a decline in blood levels of adrenal steroids, like DHEA. A low DHEA level is also associated with a high cancer risk. Royal jelly is the only nutritional agent which supplies a high density of nutrients as well as safe and natural hormones. Regular consumption boosts the cellular stores of critical nutrients as well as hormones. This may account for its anti-aging actions, because the cells must have nutrients and hormones to regenerate.

The regenerative processes of the intestines illustrate how this works. Every day billions of intestinal cells die. These cells must be replaced, otherwise disease results. The body must independently procure the nutrients necessary to rebuild these uncountable billions of cells. Procuring these nutrients is a tedious process. Commercial foods are completely depleted, so it is virtually impossible to induce regeneration from these foods. In fact, processed foods induce degeneration. Even chemical-free, farmed-raised, and organic foods fail to provide sufficient density to induce regeneration. In all of these food sources nutrients exist in relatively low density. This is why royal jelly is so valuable. It provides the building blocks needed for reconstruction. This decreases the stress on the digestive organs. The process of reconstruction now becomes easier, because, when royal jelly is consumed, the necessary nutrients are provided. Instead of the cells being forced to synthesize difficult to produce substances, like DNA and RNA, these substances are in essence "hand delivered." The DNA and RNA are required for cellular repair and may largely account for royal jelly's anti-aging action. Yet, royal jelly does more: it induces the body to produce its own genetic material. French researchers have proven that royal jelly provokes the intracellular synthesis of DNA. This compound is the very basis of life. This explains why researchers worldwide claim that royal jelly revives the body when all other therapies fail.

Some foods cause the body more work to digest than they are nutritionally worth.Thus, little nourishment is derived in the process. This is especially true of processed and refined foods. Even when the processed foods are synthetically fortified, they fail to provide the intense biological nutrition that the body craves. Eventually, due to the inadequacy of the food, key nutrients are depleted from the body, weakening the body's resistance. Yet, if this state of poor nutrition is perpetuated, the health of future generations will also be greatly weakened.

Focusing on eating to live, Americans are overfed and undernourished. It is more desirable to consume less food, while consuming mainly those which are nutrient dense. These nutrient dense foods nourish and strengthen the body, never depleting it. Thus, focusing on eating for life can radically improve life and add years of restful living to your life potential. Royal jelly is perhaps the most nutrient dense and nutrient replenishing of all foods.

Chapter 1
Wild Recipe

In many respects royal jelly is a wild food. So are other bee products, like honey, propolis, and pollen. It is also a sort of crude or unprocessed food. The lack of processing is important, because this means virtually all of the original nutrients are retained. Wild foods possess properties unavailable in commercial or farm raised foods. Thus, wild foods are the ideal type of food to consume.What's more, eating wild foods is the best defense against the greatest danger of modern times: the ingestion of genetically altered (engineered) foods.

Royal jelly is synthesized by bees, which gather the raw materials from various plants, like flowers and tree buds. Here is how it is made. The bees go into the pastures, forests, and grasslands and select certain plants to pollinate. In the process they gather pollen. The pollen is brought back to the hive and is fed to nurse bees. The nurse bees digest the pollen, and from it they produce royal jelly. The jelly is then fed to the queen.

The degree of wildness depends upon the region from which the royal jelly arises. This is because royal jelly is made from pollen, and its nutritional composition depends upon its pollen source. Thus, the ideal type of royal jelly arises from a primitive region, where natural vegetation flourishes versus that arising from a region of primarily farmland. Even so, bees collect pollen anywhere they can; there is always wild pollen in their batches.

While pollen is the raw material for making royal jelly, this is not to say that pollen and royal jelly are the same. It is impossible to achieve the same benefits from pollen as are derived from royal jelly; they are incomparable. Royal jelly is superior medicinally, because it is a predigested substance. Plus, it is fortified by the internal secretions, including the enzymes, of the nurse bees.

The benefits of a predigested food are immense. It takes energy to digest food. Royal jelly is completely digested. Thus, it is immediately used by the body. While common foods precipitate digestion, these foods may actually drain energy, because it takes energy to digest. In contrast, royal jelly activates digestion and creates energy.

The fact that royal jelly is predigested explains why it is such a rich source of enzymes. The enzymes are secreted into the royal jelly by the bees. This is also why sublingual dosing is so therapeutic, because royal jelly may be immediately utilized by the body, and sublingual dosing gets it right where it is needed: into the blood.

Royal jelly contains virtually every known nutrient. Few if any foods match its nutritional density. Liver is the closest match, but it is inferior in many respects. Thus, royal jelly may be regarded as the world's most concentrated nutritional source. Yet, it is far from a mere nutritional supplement. Royal jelly contains pharmaceutical-like chemicals with potent medicinal powers. It is an excellent source of hormones, which are found in no other food or herb. It is an unusually rich source of genetic material, that is DNA and RNA. The genetic material is critical for cellular repair as well as for the synthesis of new cells. What's more, royal jelly contains the rare neurotransmitter, acetylcholine, found in no other food. Other rare substances include globulins and hydroxy acids. Furthermore, it contains a number of unknown compounds.

Up to 4% of the weight consists of natural substances for which the function and structure are unknown, that is they defy analysis. In other words, the researchers know these substances exist, but they don't know what they are. Yet, such substances are certain to exert profound therapeutic benefits, effects which are superior to those produced by man-made drugs, which are merely synthetic chemicals.

Nutritional density

Royal jelly is the most nutrient dense of all foods. It contains all the known B vitamins. Pantothenic acid, the anti-stress vitamin, is found in an ultra dense supply. By weight royal jelly is approximately 13% protein, which makes it richer in this critical nutrient than virtually any known substance. It contains a large percentage of essential fatty acids, as much as 7%. Much of this fat content is in the form of lipids, including phospholipids and steroids. The phospholipids are essential for nerve cell regeneration. They are also used for brain cell formation. Steroids are cholesterol-like compounds with significant hormonal actions. The steroid hormones exert potent control over cellular activities. They help initiate important biological reactions. In addition, royal jelly is particularly rich in its own unique fatty acid, that is the hydroxy acid known as 10-hydroxy decanoic acid (10-HDA.) This is a monounsaturated fat similar to the type found in extra virgin olive oil. However, 10-HDA is a potent substance. It exerts a dramatic effect upon cell function. This fatty acid acts as a pre-hormone, feeding the glands so that they can make hormones on demand. 10-HDA also provides nourishment for the skin. In fact, this is a hydroxy acid, which improves the texture of the skin. Hydroxy acids help skin cells retain moisture. They also act as natural antiseptics, protecting the skin from germ attack. Plus, they aid in healing infected skin. Thus, royal jelly, with its high content of hydroxy acids, has been reported to aid in the healing of eczema, psoriasis, chronic dermatitis, and other skin disorders. Ziboh's work, published in *Lipids,* describes how hydroxy acids, like 10-HDA, act as potent anti-inflammatory agents. This may further explain the observation that royal jelly helps reverse chronic inflammatory skin diseases, like psoriasis and eczema.

Few foods are rich in vitamins A and D. The only common foods containing both of these vitamins include fatty fish, liver, and eggs. Milk must be fortified with vitamins A & D, therefore, in nature it is a poor source. However, royal jelly naturally contains both of these vitamins. It also contains vitamin E. Vitamin C is found in smaller amounts.

As mentioned previously royal jelly is exceptionally rich in a group of fats called phospholipids, the most well known of which is lecithin. Royal jelly is richer in lecithin than any other food. Inositol and choline, two components of lecithin which have B vitamin actions, are found in royal jelly in large amounts. As mentioned previously it also contains acetylcholine. This is a neurotransmitter, that is a chemical necessary for nerve conduction. Acetylcholine controls a wide range of nerve functions, including stimulation of digestion and hormone synthesis.

Perhaps most impressive is the fact that royal jelly is a rich source of naturally occurring steroids. This is what largely accounts for its creamy texture. It contains over 50 of them, including testosterone and estrogen. Estradiol is the specific type of estrogen found in royal jelly, a highly bioavailable, that is usable, form. The types of estrogen and testosterone in royal jelly are non-toxic. In fact, these natural steroids enhance male or female organ functions. The steroids in royal jelly are safe for any ailment. Thus, royal jelly is the ideal tonic for reversing hormonal disorders. A variety of conditions related to the hormone system, such as ovarian cysts, uterine spasms, fibroid tumors, PMS, menopausal syndrome, infertility, endometriosis, recurrent miscarriages, preeclampsia, impotence, adrenal insufficiency, and low libido, respond to royal jelly administration.

Royal jelly provides intensive nutrition for the queen bee. The queen is responsible for giving birth to the entire colony. Imagine this: the queen must produce as many as 2,000 eggs daily. That is more than one egg per minute. Without royal jelly, she would die from exhaustion. The fact that royal jelly keeps her strong and vital is a miracle.

The array of hormones in royal jelly alone qualifies it as a super-food. Yet, it possesses a number of other compounds which account for its vitalizing effect upon the queen as well as humans. Royden Brown described the chemical profile of royal jelly as being "very complex." This complexity largely explains how the queen bee is able to synthesize such a massive amount of eggs. These complex substances must be exceptionally potent in their ability to bolster cell function. Indeed, royal jelly offers the widest variety of nutritive substances known. A partial list of some of the key substances found in royal jelly includes:

> amino acids (some 20 total)
> vitamins
> minerals
> hydroxy acids
> phospholipids (lecithin, etc.)
> neurotransmitters (acetylcholine)
> collagen precursors
> genetic material (DNA/RNA)
> immune globulins (gamma globulin)
> albumin
> enzymes
> sex hormones
> adrenal steroids
> cellular catalysts

This is the most impressive array of biological chemicals in a single food known. These are the very substances from which cells are made and with which life proceeds. Perhaps this is why royal jelly continues to be a favorite natural tonic for all civilizations.

Royal jelly's B vitamin content alone is another reason it is a super-food. Even the intake of small amounts nourishes the body, because it is so nutrient dense. This is in contrast to the modern thinking, which is that megadoses of vitamins are needed to improve health. Perhaps this is true of synthetic vitamins, but with natural vitamins even small amounts offer important benefits. Thus, microdoses are useful, because naturally occurring vitamins are catalysts. This means only tiny amounts are needed to induce cellular regeneration. As a source of vitamins that everyone should consider the daily intake of royal jelly over a synthetic multiple vitamin. Plus, synthetic vitamins may contain harmful contaminants, including genetically altered components and solvents. The fact is the majority of multiple vitamins contain potentially toxic additives.

With the exception of liver, royal jelly offers the widest variety of B vitamins of any food. Those found in the highest amounts include pantothenic acid, riboflavin, pyridoxine, biotin, inositol, and choline. It also contains niacin, thiamine, folic acid, and vitamin B-12. Plus, it contains significant amounts of fat soluble vitamins, like vitamins A, D, and E. Its mineral content works in concert with the high content of B vitamins. Its B-6 content is of particular value. Kitzes notes in the *Journal of Nutrition* that of any food royal jelly is the best source of B-6 and that, incredibly, it is several times richer than brewer's yeast. As mentioned previously it is most well known as a source of vitamin B-5 (pantothenic acid). Pearson and Burgin describe it as "the richest known source" and that in comparison it is five times richer than liver.

For human cells royal jelly provides everything required to make energy. It is a superb source of phosphorus, which is direly needed by the cells for energy formation. Its rich niacin and riboflavin content aid in the flow of energy, since these vitamins are needed for the movement of electrons throughout the cells. As a source of zinc royal jelly is superb, containing about 53 mg per third cup. The zinc is needed for cell synthesis and repair. The fact that it is super rich in amino acids also accounts for its potent nutritional value. The amino acids are critical for the construction and repair of cells as well as for the synthesis of nuclear material. The B vitamins are the cofactors needed to initiate the reactions leading to cell building. Royal jelly is the only substance that provides a rich supply of B vitamins, minerals, and amino acids plus the nucleic acids. The latter are the genetic material that make up the nucleus of the cell. One of the nucleic acids, RNA, is also used by the body to relay genetic information throughout the cells. RNA and DNA control protein synthesis. Thus, royal jelly is the key substance for initiating the process of renewal and repair of cells, and it does so for all cells in the body.

Raw honey: the other wild recipe

Many people realize that honey is a health food. Yet, what is less well known is the fact that it is the type of honey that makes the difference in terms of how medicinal it is.

Wild and/or raw honey are the types to rely upon as natural medicines. Wild honey is completely different than the commercial types. Perhaps the wild type shouldn't even be called honey. That devalues it. Regardless, a truly wild honey is more of a medicine than a food, especially if it is unprocessed. The definition of unprocessed is that the honey is never filtered and that it is crude, that is it is unheated or minimally heated. Minimal heat is acceptable, such as up to 100 degrees; that is the temperature of a hot summer's day. Heat in excess of 100 degrees damages the delicate proteins and enzymes in raw honey, and these substances are a major part of its medicinal repertoire

The ancient Greeks used honey as a medicine. It was administered as a wound healing salve. It was also administered for infections as well as digestive disorders. Galen, who lived in the second century A.D., prescribed honey as a general health tonic. However, it was Prophet Muhammad who first popularized the value of honey, prescribing it as an outright cure for diarrhea as well as septic wounds. The Prophet routinely prescribed it as a treatment for diarrhea. A man came to him complaining of diarrhea, and he advised the intake of raw honey. The man tried it, but later returned, complaining of no benefit. The Prophet told him to take more and to keep taking it, which resulted in a cure. Here is the point: while a small amount of honey, like a few tablespoons, may eliminate diarrhea, difficult cases may require taking multiple doses using large amounts. I have used as much as a quarter cup three or four times daily for severe cases. If used consistently, it always works. If combined with natural antiseptics, the results are even superior. Note: a special combination of crude raw honey plus antiseptic essential oils is available. The brand name, Di-ARREST, is specifically designed for combating diarrhea. Take one or two tablespoons as often as needed. Di-ARREST comes in an 8 ounce bottle and is available by calling 1-800-243-5242. This is ideal to have at home or when traveling anywhere.

Modern medicine has recently confirmed the ancient findings. Researchers publishing in the *Journal of Pediatrics* determined that honey is an effective antidiarrheal for infants and that it is superior to drugs. South African doctors also treated infants, halting diarrhea where traditional therapies failed. Other traditional actions, such as the healing of wounds, have also been extensively confirmed. The *British Journal of Surgery* detailed how raw honey healed open ulcers when everything else failed. According to the researchers the wounds were regarded as incurable. The wounds were infected with drug resistant germs, that is the super-germs. Yet, incredibly, these germs were no match for the raw honey. The honey applications cured some 57 of 58 cases, a 98% cure rate. Bergman, publishing in the prestigious *American Journal of Surgery*, described how honey cured a wide range of hopelessly infected wounds. The honey therapy was effective in deep wounds, decubitus ulcers, and burns. Wounds healed more rapidly with honey than any other salve. He described its powers as "highly bactericidal." Even better results were reported by a German clinician, Dr. Zaiss of Heidelberg. He regarded honey as the most effective of all wound healing salves. Dr. Zaiss's technique was to dip strips of gauze in honey and then apply them to the wound. In most instances within 24 hours all germs were destroyed and the wounds began healing. Pain was also eliminated. Dressings were changed on a daily basis. In over a thousand cases he reported 100% results. Switzerland's Dr. Charles Brunnich relates a miracle story. His patient had a finger crushed in a grinding machine. The bone at the tip of the finger was broken off and was hanging on a flap of skin. Dr. Brunnich covered the finger with honey dressings, which held the finger together. Incredibly, the finger parts rapidly grew together and the man regained use of his finger. In another case a man had two huge boils on his back. One was surgically excised, leaving a huge ugly scar. The other was treated with raw honey. The honey cured the boil, leaving only a tiny scar. In Alberta, Canada, a 75 year old man with diabetes was bedfast in a hospital for over a year. This caused him to develop decubitus ulcers. All types of treatments were used, including a vast amount of antibiotics. None of these medical treatments worked. He was finally sent home to live (or die) with it. His family learned about the North American Herb & Spice oil of wild oregano, i.e. the Oreganol, and suggested that he use it to relieve his painful wounds. Home nurses applied the Oreganol topped with raw honey and then gauze to the draining, deeply infected wounds. In less than a month the smaller wounds were completely healed and the largest ulcer, almost 5 inches wide, was mostly healed. Incredibly, there was one "side effect": his blood sugar became normalized, strictly from the topical application of the oregano oil. Thus, he was able to reduce the dosage of his medication.

Bulgarian physicians have used raw honey extensively. Looking at respiratory diseases, including asthma, bronchitis, sinusitis, and rhinitis, they performed a huge study on some 18,000 humans. On average about 60% of all patients showed a significant improvement.

Like royal jelly, honey is predigested. Thus, it is readily processed by the digestive tract and carried into the blood. Raw honey is a valuable source of natural sugars, which may be needed by hard laborers or athletes for quick energy. It is a good source of minerals and contains only a small amount of vitamins. However, honey contains a wide range of medicinal compounds which, while only occurring in trace amounts, pack tremendous therapeutic powers. Examples of such biomedicines include flavonoids, which give honey its color, as well as enzymes, polyphenols, antiseptics, and hydrogen peroxide, the latter being a potent germicide. Like royal jelly, honey contains unknown compounds, up to 5% by weight. Many of these unknown compounds are thought to be natural antibiotics. Dark colored honeys are rich in minerals which, along with flavonoids, give them their color. However, light colored honeys, while lower in minerals, are still valuable because of the enzymes as well as flavonoids and other phytochemicals they contain.

Nutritional value

Like royal jelly, honey contains a plethora of nutrients. Many of the nutrients are found only in trace amounts. Honey's greatest value is due to its phytochemicals, in other words, its repertoire of biological medicines. Such medicinal compounds include enzymes, organic acids (e.g. malic and tartaric acids), flavonoids, polyphenols, and hormone-like molecules. However, it contains other valuable nutrients, particularly minerals. It is rather low in many of the vitamins. For instance, folic acid, pantothenic acid, vitamin C, and B-12 are often lacking. However, certain honeys are surprisingly rich in riboflavin and vitamin B-6. Russian investigators found the riboflavin content of certain honeys to be incredibly high. This may account for the yellowish-orange gleam of particular honeys, since riboflavin is a pigment of the same color. N. Yoirish, a Russian honey expert, notes that honey contains nearly as much riboflavin as chicken and 17 times more than fresh apricots, both of which are rich sources. Crude raw/unfiltered honey is the type that is particularly high in this vitamin; the riboflavin-rich pollen grains that are trapped in the honey account for much of it.

Some honeys contain only minute amounts of vitamins and minerals. The technically low amounts of standard nutrients may prove deceptive. It might be thought that such honeys offer no significant nutritional value. A study performed in Switzerland proved otherwise. The researchers studied children in poor health, dividing them into three groups. All received basically the same food with one exception: the third group was fed honey.

After a few months health factors were assessed. In contrast to the other subjects honey eaters improved dramatically and were physically superior in all parameters: in weight, physical strength, behavior, energy, and blood counts. A study performed in Austria was equally dramatic. Investigators wondered if the seemingly small amounts of minerals in honey, that is copper, iron, magnesium, and manganese, would affect blood counts. Incredibly, they did: boys fed honey showed nearly a 10% rise in the health of their blood, while those not fed honey actually showed a decline in blood health. Apparently, the types of minerals found in honey, while existing in rather small amounts, are readily used by the body. The honey-based nutrients help the body in eradicating disease. The fact that it was capable of increasing blood counts proves that honey is a potent curative agent, that is if it is unprocessed or raw.

Potassium is the mineral in honey found in highest amounts. In fact, the amounts are high enough that it can be taken, like bananas, as a type of potassium supplement. In individuals vulnerable to potassium loss two or three tablespoons daily of dark colored honey will prevent the deficiency.

Honey is an excellent source of enzymes. The types of enzymes it contains make it a highly medicinal substance. For instance, it is high in catalase and peroxidase, both of which are potent antioxidant enzymes. These enzymes have been shown to possess anti-aging and anti-toxic powers. It also contains enzymes capable of assisting digestion, particularly the digestion of starch. This means that when it is consumed with toast or fruit, these foods are digested more readily. Yoirish mentions honey as one of the richest food sources of enzymes, and he claims that it is the enzyme content that accounts for much of its healing powers. This is a reasonable assessment, since enzymes are aggressive biological molecules. They are the substances which are responsible for controlling the rate of biological reactions. This means that enzymes are catalysts. Without them, reactions fail to occur. In other words, honey without enzymes is biologically "dead". Heat readily destroys the enzymes.

Healing powers

Honey heals injuries. It is particularly valuable against burns, for which medical cures are lacking.

Usually, the thought of a severe burn strikes great fear in an individual. If such a catastrophe occurs, it is crucial that the individual understands the powers of raw honey. Honey's potent action in healing burns has been proven by modern science. New Zealand's Dr. Peter Molan, who has researched honey for over 20 years, claims that as a burn salve it is superior to any drug. In England honey is being used in burn wards. Dr. M. Subrahanyam, a British surgeon, has successfully cured burns in hospitalized patients with raw honey. The honey worked nine times better than the drugs. In fact, the honey significantly reduced scarring, as well as pain, as illustrated by the following case history: Mr. Z. was the cleaning man for my clinic. He claimed to be a part time handyman, so when his drain became plugged at home, he attempted to fix it. Powdered drain cleaner failed, so he attempted to unscrew the pipes. The problem was, the pipes were full of drain cleaner, so when he released the seal, drain cleaner splattered on his forearm. He developed a massive chemical burn and his forearm immediately became severely inflamed and blistered. After being evaluated the hospital sent him home with no hope for improvement.When I first saw him, he was in excruciating pain. I treated him with crude, raw honey along with aloe vera cream using repetitive applications. The honey/aloe dressings eliminated the pain. After two weeks of this aggressive treatment there was only minimal scarring, and he regained full use of his arm.

Raw or wild honey is an exceptionally valuable salve. It is also a relatively inexpensive one. It may be applied to virtually any external wound and is certainly safer, as well as more effective, than anything else in the medicine cabinet. For medicinal purposes use only guaranteed raw or wild honey. Simply apply it on the involved site and cover; leave for 12 to 24 hours. Apply additional poultices as often as needed. Usually, results are observed within 48 hours. Wounds/injuries for which raw honey is curative include:

> cuts
> bruises
> abrasions
> warts
> cold sores
> ulcerations
> swollen or varicose veins
> burns
> radiation injury
> chemical injury
> boils
> pimples
> abscesses
> infected cuts
> contusions
> abrasions
> herpes outbreaks
> animal bites
> insect bites

It is important to know what is the definition of raw honey. This is the only medicinal type. Commercial honey is somewhat valuable as a sweetener, but it fails to provide the potent therapeutic action of the crude raw types. Here are key questions to utilize to determine if the honey you buy is medicinal:

- Does the honey sink to the bottom of a cup of hot water?
- Is it difficult to dissolve, in other words, must you stir it repeatedly to dissolve it?
- Does it stick aggressively to utensils and is exceptionally difficult to remove?
- Is it of a thick consistency?
- Is it guaranteed to be raw or unheated (if it doesn't say so on the label, call the maker and request a verbal confirmation; some culinary honeys, while raw and unfiltered, do not make the label claim)?
- When refrigerated, does it readily crystallize?
- Is it unfiltered?
- Is it significantly more costly than the commercial type?
- Does the honey have a sort of glow to it, a bit of a glimmer, as if it is producing energy versus having a dull lifeless appearance?

The aforementioned are dependable rules to ascertain the quality and purity of honey. Always follow these rules to be sure the honey you buy is of the highest quality. Be willing to pay extra for superior material. In fact, an inexpensive price is nearly always a signal of inferior quality. Incredibly, certain unscrupulous purveyors corrupt their honey by diluting it with sugary syrups and water. Through buying only medicinal grade honey, your health and physique will benefit. So will your longevity.

The term "raw" must also be defined. Technically, raw means no heat is applied. With honey the main issue is that no heat over 100 degrees must be applied. That is because temperatures above

100 degrees destroy the natural enzymes in the honey, which are important therapeutic agents. The enzymes aid digestion, plus they assist in wound healing.

There is another rule for determining the quality of honey: the diet of the bees. In an effort to keep up with demand and to stay financially competitive, modern beekeepers have adopted an abhorrent practice: they feed the bees sugar, primarily during the winter. Normally, bees eat their own honey to survive the winter. That reduces the beekeeper's profits. So, the bees are fed corn syrup or refined sugar syrup. This is done so that the honey normally consumed by the bees can be sold. Such a practice certainly corrupts the honey, causing it to lose its medicinal powers, and it also corrupts the bees. Bees eat nectar, not sugar. Bees that are fed sugar will be unhealthy. The honey and/or royal jelly they produce will be inferior. That is why there are so many diseases and mite infestations in bees today.

Old fashioned beekeepers are a disciplined lot. They don't succumb to market demands. They known their honey is valuable, because they know it is a medicine. They will not sell it cheap, because they know there will always be a demand for it. These beekeepers, who are becoming rare, know the health of their bees is dependent upon allowing them to consume their natural forage. They would never feed their bees sugar, no matter what the demands or circumstances. These are the makers of the truly raw and wild honeys. Only these types of honeys are found on the Web site MedicinalHoneys.com or call 1-800-243-5242.

The powers of bee propolis

Propolis, another one of the bees' wild productions, is a brownish colored substance found on the inside and outside of bee hives. Bees use it to glue their hives together. It is a sticky resin derived primarily from the buds of various trees. Yet, its function is beyond that of a mere glue: it is needed to keep the hive sterile. Bee propolis is one of the most powerful natural antiseptics known. It also possesses significant antiinflammatory and anesthetic properties. What's more, it is a potent antioxidant, far more powerful than, for instance, vitamins E or C. This vast array of properties is explained by a simple fact: propolis is perhaps the most dense source of plant flavonoids known. The plant flavonoids exert drug-like actions on human cells. In other words, they are natural pharmaceutical agents. Flavonoids are powerful antiinflammatory agents, plus they possess anti-allergy, anti-pain, and anti-infection powers. According to Jean Monro, Ph.D., plant flavonoids are completely safe for human consumption.

Propolis has been used as a natural medicine for thousands of years. It is perhaps most famous for its wound healing properties. In this respect its actions are dramatic. I have seen seemingly impossible to cure wounds healed in a matter of hours after topical or internal use. The wound healing properties may be attributed to several mechanisms. It is a resin, and, thus, it exerts a glue-like action on the tissues. It is a natural antibiotic and, thus, by killing germs it speeds healing. Furthermore, by action of its rich supply of bioflavonoids it is an anti-inflammatory agent, and, thus, it exerts cortisone-like actions on the tissues.

Propolis' antibiotic action has been extensively researched. Test tube studies show it kills a wide range of bacteria, including E. coli and staph. In Japan it is used as a natural antibiotic and is a popular cold/flu treatment. The Japanese have also popularized propolis as a cancer treatment.

The Japanese have made a thorough study of the medicinal properties of this substance. Their studies confirm that propolis is essentially an herbal drug. For instance, propolis fights pain. Doctors at the Tokyo Medical and Dental University found that the internal consumption of propolis blocked pain better than aspirin. I have used a mixture of bee propolis plus essential oils against pain and found it highly effective.

Dr. T. Matsuno, one of the world's premier authorities on propolis and author of the book *Propolis: Its Pharmacology and Therapeutic Effects,* has discovered dozens of valuable properties for this substance. He describes how propolis reversed skin inflammation better than drugs. This illustrates the potential value of propolis in the treatment of inflammatory skin diseases, like psoriasis, eczema, and dermatitis. In fact, Dr. Matsuno lists a variety of skin diseases which responded to propolis therapy. However, his major expertise was in the treatment of cancer. He found that propolis was an effective secondary treatment in a wide range of malignancies.

Dr. Matsuno proved that propolis is a potent substance and that it supercedes many drugs. Using diagnostic equipment, like ultrasound, microscopes, and x-rays, he provided pictorial proof that propolis offers significant curative powers. The conditions in which Dr. Matsuno found propolis to be effective include cancer, dermatitis, scabies, hepatitis, diabetes, pyorrhea, herpetic infections, and hemorrhoids. He describes dozens of case histories in his highly technical but informative book. The immense safety of propolis is illustrated by its effects on an individual with hepatitis: it normalized the elevated liver enzyme levels. However, the positive results Dr. Matsuno described in cancer are perhaps most impressive. Cancer chemotherapy is harsh, leading to the destruction of healthy as well as diseased tissue. Propolis aids in the battle against cancer by helping the body destroy cancer cells without damaging human cells. He described a case where an individual with incurable liver cancer went into remission as a result of propolis therapy.

Polish investigators discovered potential novel uses for propolis. They found it to be highly biologically active and that it readily kills a wide range of germs. It was even able to halt the growth of parasites, specifically protozoans. They also found that it stimulates tissue regeneration, even aiding in bone growth.

Propolis is perhaps the most effective of all natural pain killers. German physician, Bent Havesteen formerly with Keil University, explains why: it contains a type of natural aspirin. The aspirin in bee propolis is non-toxic.

It has been reported that propolis is such an effective wound healing agent that it even heals radiation burns. Yugoslavian researchers investigated this via a double blind study. Those who took propolis noticeably improved—some wounds even "disappeared"—while those who took a fake pill failed to improve. Russian scientists at Children's Hospital in St. Petersburg offer an explanation for these healing powers: they claim propolis contains a substance capable of regenerating skin cells. They found that in youngsters with infected skin propolis applications created new skin cells. The positive effects were most prominent in infants, for which it is completely safe.

The Russians have also proven that propolis is an immune aid. They found that the ingestion of propolis boosts the ability of white blood cells to kill germs. Dr. N. P. Iojris found another benefit: a potent antiviral action. The Russians discovered that propolis induced a rise in antiviral proteins and antibodies. Thus, it greatly enhances the natural antiviral defenses.

There is a potential problem with propolis: lead contamination. Be sure the propolis you use is certified free of unacceptable levels of lead.

A special emulsion of propolis is now available. Known as Prop-O-Heal this is a combination of lead-free propolis and edible essential oils. It is emulsified in a base of crude extra virgin olive oil. Prop-O-Heal is an excellent source of antiinflammatory and wound healing flavonoids, which are naturally occurring in the propolis. It is made by a special process, which makes the active ingredients highly available to the tissues. Prop-O-Heal is easy to use: simply take a few drops under the tongue as often as needed. It is also available in a topical cream. The cream is useful for reversing aging of the skin as well as skin injury. It is particularly valuable for burns, including sunburn. It may also be used to heal tissues internally. Its broad-spectrum healing properties make it useful in a variety of illnesses, including traumatic pain, chronic pain, inflammatory disorders, liver disease, intestinal disorders, and chronic infection.

Propolis is difficult to absorb. However, emulsification in fat aids in absorption, plus it makes it easier to use on skin. Emulsified propolis is a tremendously effective wound healing agent. It exerts this action whether applied topically or taken internally.

Case history:

A 43 year old male developed cracks at the corners of his mouth after a bad case of the flu. The cracks were exceptionally painful. He tried to heal them with a variety of compounds with marginal results. After suffering with the cracks for several days he applied Prop-O-Heal. He felt a sort of tingling sensation; the pain relief was immediate. Within an hour the cracks were noticeably improved. Within 24 hours they were completely healed.

Prop-O-Heal is relatively new, so it may not be available in stores. It is a superb substance for supporting the natural healing process. For more information call 1-800-243-5242.

Chapter 2
The Research

Royal jelly has been researched extensively in the lab, in test tubes, in animals, and in humans. Because of this intensive research there are extensive claims regarding its curative powers. There is also a certain degree of skepticism. In particular, medical doctors are skeptical about it. Thus, they usually disregard any claims, as well as research, regarding its efficacy.

It is reasonable to expect that claims should be scrutinized, as long as the scrutiny is unbiased. The problem is that it is expected that natural substances should be subjected to rigorous scrutiny, even while modern medical counterparts are accepted wholesale. Aspirin is an excellent example. While this drug originates from a natural substance, the bark of the willow tree, the current form, that is synthetic aspirin, can be toxic. The crude type, that is the herbal type, from white willow bark is non-toxic. There are no deaths on record from white willow bark consumption. There are thousands of deaths from synthetic aspirin consumption. Certainly, natural products should be properly evaluated, primarily for safety. There should be substantial proof for their efficacy.

With the majority of natural substances it is unnecessary to spend millions of dollars on double blind research. The purpose of double blind research is to attempt to prove if a therapy has value (or potential harsh effects). The efficacy of royal jelly is already proven by the test of time and by millions of human cases. Plus, hundreds of scientific studies have been performed, confirming that royal jelly is indeed one of those rare elixirs that greatly impacts human health—without untoward effects. Even if millions of dollars were spent researching royal jelly, it will only confirm what is already known: that it helps alleviate a wide range of complaints and even reverses certain diseases outright.

Safety is one of the biggest concerns regarding natural substances. No one wants to take something that might have side effects. Royal jelly is a food, and it has a safety profile similar to other natural foods. It is completely edible and is safe for all ages, including babies. Royal jelly therapy results in a wide range of positive results, including the opportunity to feel tremendously healthy like never before. Quality and reliability of the raw material is also a significant concern. Royal jelly is a rare substance. Inexpensive forms are likely to be inferior in quality. Check with the manufacturer to be sure the quality and purity are guaranteed.

While royal jelly is one of the safest of all nutritional supplements, there is a small chance for allergic reactions. Certain individuals may be allergic to bee stings. Occasionally, such an individual might also be allergic to bee products, including honey, bee pollen, and royal jelly. In this instance, proceed with a bit of caution. Start taking a small amount, like a tenth of a capsule or a drop of the stabilized liquid. For individuals who are severely allergic to bee stings or pollen it may be necessary to avoid royal jelly completely. However, royal jelly is such a valuable substance that, ideally, everyone should attempt to benefit from it. Taking tiny amounts and then gradually increasing it is a method to help determine if it can be tolerated. Yet, it must be emphasized that royal jelly is one of the safest of all nutritional supplements. For instance, it is safer to consume than the majority of common foods or beverages. Did you know that breaded foods, such as fried chicken, chicken nuggets, fish sticks, fried mushrooms, etc., contain a known carcinogen? Were you aware that tap water, or the water at a restaurant, contains substances which damage the arteries? Royal jelly is safe. Use it as you need it, and use it in whatever quantity is necessary to achieve the desired results.

The reason that royal jelly is so unique is that it is both safe and effective. Many herbals or natural medicines are effective but they cannot be taken in unlimited quantities. Royal jelly is a food-like medicine, so it can be consumed in relatively large amounts without concern.

Research has proven that royal jelly aids human health in numerous ways. No one is certain precisely how it works. In fact, it was Dr. A Saenz of the Pasteur Institute who proclaimed that royal jelly possesses "remarkable and mysterious" healing properties.

The health enhancing properties of royal jelly are far more significant than those resulting from drug therapy. It is useful in virtually all disciplines. Here are the benefits as categorized within the various medical specialties:

Geriatrics (Anti-aging)

Dozens of studies indicate that royal jelly blocks the aging process. This benefit is seen both with topical and internal use. Topically, royal jelly keeps the skin supple, that is it helps the skin retain moisture. It also provides nourishment, helping regenerate skin cells. Royal jelly contains steroid hormones, which eliminate swelling and inflammation. Taken internally, it is such a potent tonic that it fights aging in every organ. Dr. Saenz emphasizes the fact that royal jelly is the richest source of a potent anti-aging factor: pantothenic acid. This vitamin is one of the most versatile anti-aging substances known. This is because it helps block aging within the skin, plus it keeps the adrenal glands in optimal health. When the adrenal glands fail, aging accelerates greatly. In animals length of life was increased merely by adding pantothenic acid to food.

Mental diseases of the elderly often improve dramatically after royal jelly therapy. Binet noted that royal jelly is usually effective in reversing the mental disturbances seen in senility diseases. Royden Brown describes a case of Parkinson's disease which dramatically improved. German doctors also used it for this condition, describing several cases of remissions.

Royal jelly strengthens the function of the nervous system, especially the sympathetic nervous system, which is highly dysfunctional in senility diseases. It also improves adrenal function. The adrenal glands control blood sugar levels, and senility diseases are associated with disordered blood sugar metabolism.

The elderly are in dire need of hormonal support. When the body ages, the levels of hormones drop significantly. This lack of hormones leads to tissue aging, including aging of the skin. Royal jelly is nature's most potent hormone supplement. Plus, the types of hormones it contains are completely safe. When taken by the elderly, it gently boosts hormone levels, providing much needed strength, energy, and vitality.

Royal jelly contains a number of vitamins which possess anti-aging powers. Pantothenic acid itself fights aging. Apparently, the type found naturally in royal jelly works more aggressively than the synthetic type. This is evidenced by the fact that rather small doses of royal jelly appear to impede the aging process, and these doses contain only tiny amounts of the vitamin, far less than would be found in, for instance, the typical multiple vitamin. In food pantothenic acid is difficult to procure. The richest sources are organ meats, germs of grains, fresh red meat, egg yolk, salmon, and peanut butter. Other than perhaps peanut butter and red meat most of these foods are neglected on the average daily menu. Plus, with the elderly red meat and egg consumption is limited, because of inability to chew and dietary restrictions. Elderly individuals on a strict low fat diet are routinely deficient in pantothenic acid. Thus, the majority of elderly individuals on the standard diets for heart disease are severely deficient, since pantothenic acid is found primarily in fatty foods. Royal jelly provides micro-doses of the vitamin, but, incredibly, this is a sufficient amount to correct the deficiency symptoms. Plus, in contrast to the type found in the typical vitamin pills, the pantothenic acid found in royal jelly is readily absorbed, because it is 100% natural and highly bioavailable.

A variety of investigators claim that royal jelly reverses mental symptoms, including depression, anxiety, nervousness, memory loss, and insomnia. This may be largely due to its rich content of the neurotransmitter of acetylcholine, which it contains in amounts as high as one mg per gram. The levels in the nervous system of this substance decline dramatically during aging. The direct intake of this neurotransmitter through the consumption of royal jelly may account for the rather dramatic improvement in mental capacity observed by some researchers. Ideally, sublingual dosing provides the most potent means of replenishing this rare substance.

After studying the anti-aging powers of royal jelly Dr. Saenz came to this conclusion, "Royal jelly allows man to recover his biological balance and confront aging with optimism and serenity.... Nature has created a *genuine panacea* for the aged or, to put it simply, for the adult who wishes to extend the limits of the natural aging process." (italics mine) This is confirmed by researchers at the University of Southern California, who claim that royal jelly is one of the few substances capable of overriding the genetic clock, blocking the inevitable: cellular aging.

Pediatrics

Royal jelly is of lifesaving importance in pediatrics. It should be a mainstay in hospital wards, especially in neonatology. All premature babies should receive it. If given preventively, it would essentially obliterate postnatal infections. Plus, it would eliminate minor conditions such as neonatal jaundice, cradle cap, and colic. Since it is completely harmless, the only possible result is positive: increased growth, improved immunity, and stronger constitution. As described by Irene Stein in her book, *Royal Jelly, Guide to Nature's Richest Health Food*, royal jelly was found to cure malnutrition in babies, including premature ones. Doctors at the University of Florence fed 42 babies royal jelly with astounding results. All of the babies gained weight, plus their immune systems were strengthened and their red blood cell counts increased. These are tremendously positive changes, which are unmatched by any medication. Dr. Allen and B. Lust in their book, *The Royal Jelly Miracle*, describe how undernourished babies were given royal jelly. Within two weeks all of the babies became plump, with full return of their appetites.

Royal jelly is one of the few nutritional supplements that is safe for infants. It nourishes them to such an intensive degree that the results are readily evident. Royal jelly should be a mainstay of treatment for any infant with poor growth, developmental problems, impaired immunity, and poor appetite. Yet, it should also be given to healthy babies, so that they become as strong as possible.

Children respond equally as well as infants. Italian researchers found that children with failure to thrive rapidly improved with royal jelly therapy. Appetite became vigorous and growth was accelerated. Teenagers with stunted growth also responded, growing rapidly to their natural height and weight. This is the ideal tonic for the child or teenager with poor eating habits. The appetite quickly becomes more vigorous, and the desire for healthy foods is dramatically enhanced.

Cardiology

Hardening of the arteries, angina, heart failure, and heart disease have been reversed with royal jelly. Human studies have proven that royal jelly, even in small quantities, positively affects cholesterol and triglyceride counts. Broadhurst reports that as little as 100 mg of royal jelly lowers cholesterol by as much as 14%, a greater reduction than is typically achieved with garlic. Triglycerides were lowered by as much as 10%. Obviously, higher doses would result in even a greater decline. For individuals with high cholesterol/triglyceride levels a reasonable dose might be about 1000 mg daily or about two capsules of Royal Kick daily. Animal studies have shown that royal jelly helps reverse hardening of the arteries. Royal jelly is also a tonic for the heart. It helps improve heart rhythm, plus it increases its pumping power. Dr. H. W. Schimdt of Germany found that elderly patients with hardening of the arteries improved as a result of royal jelly treatments. Dr. A. Saenz of the Pasteur Institute found that royal jelly greatly strengthens the arteries. He described cases of individuals with abnormal blood lipids and evidence of hardening of the arteries improving dramatically after taking royal jelly.

Royal jelly is an effective nerve tonic. It helps relax agitated nerves, inducing a sort of calm state. The heart and arteries are controlled by the nervous system. Stress and anger may precipitate heart disease. Thus, by combating the toxic effects of stress, royal jelly may prove helpful in reversing a variety of cardiovascular conditions, including high blood pressure, angina, heart failure, and coronary heart disease.

Obstetrics and Gynecology

Royal jelly is a natural source of estrogen and progesterone. Thus, it offers immense utility in this specialty. A wide range of conditions can potentially benefit. One reason for its universal value is that royal jelly is a natural source of steroid hormones. The steroids control a wide range of female functions, including ovulation, menstruation, fertilization, temperature control, sexual arousal, and libido. Thus, disorders of the female glands are often due to a deficiency and/or imbalance in steroid hormone production and/or metabolism. Both estrogen and progesterone are steroids.

Breast problems readily respond to royal jelly therapy. This is particularly true of fibrocystic breast disease and/or swollen/sore breasts. Usually, an improvement is noted within a week or two. Studies have documented reversal of breast cysts, soreness, and inflammation plus the unexpected benefit of improved appearance and increased girth. Note: women who already have large breasts don't have an aggravation. Apparently, this action is seen only in women with insufficient breast development.

Royal jelly is reportedly a cure for low libido. It boosts the desire for sex by increasing stamina and vitality. However, it also helps induce a sort of natural female "love reflex." Thus, females who regularly take royal jelly tend to have a greater than normal desire to initiate love making. What's more, the response to male arousal increases as do the vaginal secretions. Royal jelly is likely to make love-making a more pleasant and powerful experience. For exceptional results take a fortified type of royal jelly, that is royal jelly plus pantothenic acid, an hour or two before attempting relations. Also, take it regularly, like 2 to 6 capsules every morning. Also, just before relations take sublingual royal jelly, e.g. Royal Oil, about a half teaspoon. This will create additional arousal and stamina.

Oncology

A number of studies have proven that royal jelly protects the body from cancer. The effects are so dramatic that it is shocking that cancer doctors are so unfamiliar with it. Lust reports that Greek physicians found it useful against leukemia. Canadian researchers proved that mice fed royal jelly became immune from cancer development. Turkish physicians at the University of Cukurova determined that a small amount of royal jelly was highly effective in childhood malignancies, including leukemia and lymphoma. All of the children improved: they gained weight, their appetites became vigorous, and their immune systems functioned better. In 1994 French investigators found that the active ingredient of royal jelly, 10-HDA, possesses anti-cancer powers. This compound improved the ability of white blood cells to destroy tumor cells. This elevates royal jelly to a rare status: It is one of the few compounds which, if taken regularly, will protect the body from cancerous degeneration.

Perhaps the most valuable arena in oncology for royal jelly is in support of individuals undergoing chemotherapy. Here, royal jelly is lifesaving. It helps rejuvenate the body which has been subjected to this gruesome therapy. It revives shocked tissues, increasing the resistance to infection and stress. It regenerates the appetite and relieves stomach pain. It attempts to rebuild an immune system battered by harsh poisons. One women relates how she underwent both surgery and chemotherapy, which disabled her immune system. Chemotherapy directly destroys white blood cells. As she had little natural defense left, she developed a persistent cold and had no energy. Soon after beginning royal jelly therapy her cold disappeared. She was able to function again, having enough energy to work normally. The point is royal jelly is one of the few reliable and safe tonics for individuals recovering from chemotherapy. Take it as a supportive therapy. It is likely to ease much of the distress associated with this toxic therapy. It may give the body a chance to rebuild, to regain the healthy cell and organ function it needs to survive.

Gastroenterology

A number of physicians have observed that royal jelly heals ulcers. Perhaps this universal observation is due to the fact that it is a rich source of pantothenic acid, a vitamin well known to induce healing. It may be royal jelly's cortisone-like action that is responsible. Regardless of the mechanism of action the fact is royal jelly greatly aids in the healing of stomach and intestinal ulcers. Plus, it is safe to take with medications, because it is merely a food.

Disorders of the intestines respond well to royal jelly. This substance greatly nourishes the colonic and intestinal cells, which induce rebuilding and regeneration. Stress is a major cause of colitis attacks. This is directly related to weak adrenal function. The direct action of royal jelly on the adrenal glands may aid in reversing this condition. Thus, the regular intake of royal jelly increases the tolerance to stress, which reduces the incidence of stress-induced colitis attacks. This means that the individual is better able to cope. What's more, by boosting adrenal function royal jelly helps diminish toxic allergic reactions, which are a major cause of colitis attacks. Royal jelly's pantothenic acid content helps nourish the bowel wall. This vitamin is needed to strengthen the tone of the colonic muscles. The result is a reduction in cramping and spasms. Thus, royal jelly operates through a variety of mechanisms to help normalize the function of the colon.

Royal jelly provides nutrients in a predigested form. This means that little or no digestive work is needed to process them. The nutrients are easily absorbed into the blood or lymph. Thus, it is the ideal nutritional supplement for individuals with impaired or feeble digestion.

Commonly, cancer patients suffer from cachexia, a severe lack of appetite. This lack of appetite is caused by the cancer and also by the typical treatment. Royal Oil, a stabilized form of raw royal jelly, both nourishes the body and increases the appetite. Small doses held under the tongue taken repeatedly would be highly beneficial. Squirt it under the tongue and hold as long as possible, then swallow the remainder with whatever liquid is desired. For a comforting and nutritious tonic a teaspoon or so may be added to a cup of hot water and sipped as a tea.

Rheumatology

A number of studies have been done using royal jelly to treat arthritis. Usually, the results are positive. Carlton Fredericks, Ph.D., states in *Food Facts and Fallacies* that royal jelly and pantothenic acid help reverse arthritic symptoms. They do so by strengthening the adrenal glands, which are responsible for fighting pain and inflammation. The adrenal glands produce natural cortisone, which is the body's main anti-inflammatory substance. Plus, royal jelly contains pain-killing substances, including hydroxy acids and natural cortisone.

In the 1960s English physicians performed a rather large study on arthritics. Using a combination of royal jelly and pantothenic acid, they monitored symptoms and blood vitamin levels. As the levels in the blood of pantothenic acid rose, so responded the arthritic symptoms. In all subjects within 28 days there was a definite improvement, and in a number of patients pain was completely eliminated. These individuals had dozens of symptoms of rheumatism. Incredibly, in many instances all of the symptoms disappeared. The patients were followed for over a year, and as long as they continued to take the royal jelly and pantothenic acid treatment they remained in remission.

Neurology

Like all other organs the brain and spinal cord, as well as the peripheral nerves, are dependent upon proper nutrition. In this respect royal jelly is a boon. It provides a wide array of nutrients required by the brain and nerves for survival. German and French physicians have reported that royal jelly seems to halt aging of the brain. Germany's Dr. H. W. Schmidt has found that it reverses senility diseases. In some instances, Parkinson's disease may be ameliorated, and royal jelly is known to reduce or eliminate Parkinsonian tremors. It is the ideal nutritional supplement for stroke victims. This is because it provides a plethora of nutrients direly needed for healing brain tissue. Dr. R. Allen reports in his book *The Royal Jelly Miracle* that cantankerous elderly people tend to become calm from royal jelly therapy. In other words, the royal jelly treatments appeared to induce a balance in nerve function.

Royal jelly improves the body's ability to tolerate sugar.

Recent evidence indicates that poor sugar metabolism accelerates aging, especially of brain cells. After examining the brains of individuals with senility diseases researchers discovered that excessive levels of sugar lead to a phenomenon known as cross-linking. What happens is that the sugar disrupts the proteins of the brain cells causing them, in essence, to become stuck together. This ultimately causes the cells to die. A high intake of sugar is a major aging factor in respect to mental health.

Royal jelly enhances the body's ability to metabolize sugar. Plus, it decreases the excessive cravings for sweets. This is far from a license to continue eating sweets. If you have brown spots on your skin, this is one of the symptoms of cross-linking damage. Brown spots indicate that internal and external damage has occurred. It is largely reversible with appropriate dietary changes plus anti-aging tonics such as royal jelly, rosemary extracts, extracts of oregano, oil of myrtle, oil of lavender, etc. Reduce the intake of sugar, and take royal jelly. Also, topically, use an anti-aging essential oil formula. Skin Clenz, which contains oils of oregano, rosemary, lavender, and myrtle, is available. Simply apply to the involved area twice per day. Add a few drops of Skin Clenz to your favorite anti-aging or beauty cream. To order call 1-800-243-5242. This, along with the internal consumption of royal jelly, is the best prescription for preventing cross-linking.

Infectious diseases

There is an extensive amount of data documenting royal jelly's potent action on strengthening the immune system. Research indicates that royal jelly is a general tonic, that is it enhances a wide range of immune parameters. Regular consumption improves the ability of white blood cells to cleanse the body of toxins, germs, and even cancer cells. There is yet another potency: royal jelly contains substances which kill germs. Thus, it offers two mechanisms of action: direct antiseptic powers plus immune boosting actions. In 1978 a fascinating study was done by Eastern European doctors. They found that royal jelly inhibits the growth of herpes viruses, the type which causes cold sores and genital lesions. In 1998 Brazilian researchers determined that royal jelly is antifungal and that it halts the growth of skin fungi. Egyptian physicians (1995) discovered that royal jelly exerts a potent antiseptic action against certain difficult to kill bacteria, like staph and E. coli. Part of the reason for this power is that it is a highly acidic substance, which inhibits bacterial growth. Another reason for this power was recently uncovered by the Chinese, who are experts in the therapeutic use of royal jelly. Dr. Xiao and colleagues, publishing in *Acta Entomologica Sinica*, discovered that royal jelly contains a powerful protein that decimates germs. Dr. Xiao describes the protein, actually a peptide, as "strongly inhibitory."

French investigators (1994) made an important finding about how royal jelly strengthens immunity: it increases the killing power of the white blood cells. The cells which were fed royal jelly aggressively destroyed invaders, producing large amounts of a natural germicide called "superoxide anion." What's more, the French researchers found a potent immune boosting substance in royal jelly. It is a compound which stimulates the synthesis of genetic material. This compound was also found to improve the cancer killing power of immune cells. The royal jelly extracts were able to induce the production of white blood cells, an incredible response which even the most potent drugs fail to match. Apparently, fatty acid bound derivatives worked the best, which illustrates the value of taking a fatty emulsion of royal jelly, e.g. Royal Oil. This is a combination of high potency liquid royal jelly plus crude pumpkinseed oil. The emulsification with natural fatty acids increases the absorption of royal jelly compounds, plus it apparently helps activate them, so they can properly nourish the cells. Thus, the crude/raw royal jelly/fatty acid combination is superior to the regular liquid royal jelly in terms of biological completeness. Also, since it is stabilized it doesn't require freezing. Royal Oil is a specialty nutritional supplement and may be found in higher quality health food stores, or to order directly call 1-800-243-5242.

There is yet another arena in which royal jelly is productive: recovery from infections. Major infections wreak havoc on the body. Due to the weakened state of the body, recovery may be slow or impaired. The infections place great demands upon the adrenal glands which subsequently are often severely depleted. What's more, severe infections   induce a wide range of nutritional deficiencies, including deficiencies of zinc, vitamin A, and vitamin C. Royal jelly is particularly rich in zinc and vitamin A, both of which are readily utilized by the recovering immune system. Royal jelly's value in the regeneration of the immune system is a result of its ability to strengthen the adrenal glands. The regular intake of royal jelly may significantly reduce the recovery time after serious infections and perhaps prevent further infections.

Royal jelly is an immune tonic. It is completely safe for all ages. It provides key nutrients for immune cell health and also aids in immune cell reproduction. Its highly specialized fatty acid, decanoic acid, greatly aids in the production of powerful immune cells. This mechanism of action, that is the induction of the synthesis of white blood cells, is unknown in any other food. Plus, it is the only known natural source of gamma globulin, which is desperately needed by white blood cells to kill germs. In particular, gamma globulin helps protect the intestines from allergic toxicity as well as infections. These various and significant immune boosting powers of royal jelly explain why it is useful in virtually every known disease.

Chapter 3
The Diseases

Royal jelly is beneficial for hundreds of illnesses. This is because it strengthens the cells, increasing their resistance against disease. Plus, it regenerates cells, bringing new life to the tissues. Thus, it is one of those rare substances that may prove useful for the alteration of virtually any disease. At a minimum it provides supportive nutrition. At a maximum it helps the body in its recovery process.

Royal jelly is a regenerative substance, and, because it is nutrient dense, it is supportive therapy for numerous conditions. It should not be touted as a sudden or miraculous cure but as a nutritive tonic, that is a tonic to aid the body's natural healing processes. However, the following are conditions proven to respond to this invaluable substance. Evidence for the following is derived from scientific research as well as human case histories.

Acne

This condition, so unsightly, is largely due to nutritional imbalances. It is also related to hormonal disturbances. Teenagers are faced with sudden fluctuations in hormone levels. If they are malnourished and/or if they eat processed foods, the hormonal imbalances may be severe enough to precipitate acne. This is why royal jelly is so valuable, since it is a tremendously rich source of nutrients as well as naturally occurring hormones. It is the internal consumption that is most productive. The regular intake reduces the desire for junk foods and improves the appetite for healthy foods.

Royal jelly offers an additional benefit: it exerts therapeutic actions on the skin. The skin is normally acidic, and this acidic nature protects the skin ducts from bacteria and other germs. If the pH of the skin is disturbed, the skin is more readily invaded. Royal jelly is a highly acidic substance, in fact, it is the best naturally occurring source of hydroxy acids, the ones commonly used in skin creams. The positive actions occur whether it is applied topically or taken internally. Regular use greatly improves the health of the skin, as is manifested by a decrease in blemishes, improved thickness, improved texture, and better color.

Treatment protocol

For mild to moderate acne take 2 to 4 capsules of Royal Kick every morning with or without food. Take also stabilized liquid royal jelly (e.g. Royal Oil), 1/2 tsp. in the morning under the tongue. For severe acne take Royal Kick, 6 capsules every morning with or without meals, along with 1/2 tsp. of the Royal Oil, in the morning and at noon under the tongue. Note: the Royal Oil is a special royal jelly formula fortified with cold pressed pumpkinseed oil and natural antioxidants. It is a completely natural formula and is significantly more potent than the commercial type. Plus, it is stabilized, meaning there is no need for refrigeration. What's more, in contrast to the bitter or acidic taste of commercial royal jelly, the Royal Oil is pleasant tasting. Children love its wonderful taste and creamy texture. Also, as a natural antiseptic take oil of wild oregano (Oreganol), a few drops under the tongue once or twice daily.

Apply the oil to any swollen or infected lesions. Add oil of oregano (i.e. the Oreganol wild oregano oil blend) to soaps and facial cleansers.

Addictions

This term usually signifies the use of street drugs and alcohol. Yet, there are hundreds of other substances which are highly addictive. A partial list includes pharmaceutical drugs, diet pills, refined sugar, cigarettes, chewing tobacco, chocolate, coffee, and wine. Yet, there are few substances that offer universal support regardless of the addiction. Royal jelly is one of the few substances that reliably works for a wide range of addictions. In some instances even individuals who are hopelessly addicted are cured. The regular consumption of royal jelly offers hope for the hopeless. In her book on royal jelly Stein describes a case of Valium addiction which was nearly completely reversed with royal jelly therapy.

People with addictions often believe that the problem is primarily mental. While there is a significant mental component, the physical component is perhaps even more critical. For the addiction to be thoroughly cured this physical component must be aggressively addressed. Royal jelly aids in this process by strengthening the organs, such as the adrenal and thyroid glands, which help the body cope with the addiction recovery process. When the adrenals are strong, the cravings for addictive substances are significantly diminished. If you have a severe addiction, do not lose hope. The powers of royal jelly will come to the rescue.

Treatment protocol

Take large amounts of crude royal jelly (e.g. Royal Kick) several times daily. Also, use the Royal Oil aggressively; take it whenever you need energy, stamina, or mental balance. The secret is to use it frequently, that is as often as it is needed to produce the desired results.

Adrenal insufficiency

This illness rapidly responds to royal jelly treatment. The royal jelly addresses precisely the cause: a lack of the production of steroid hormones. Signs and symptoms of adrenal weakness include exhaustion, irritability, panic attacks, depression, anxiety, muscular weakness, fatigue, headache, chronic back pain, dizziness, cravings for sugar or salt, and inability to cope. Adrenal weakness is directly related to a deficiency in pantothenic acid, of which royal jelly is the richest source.

Treatment protocol

Depending upon the degree of deficiency, large amounts may be needed. Initially, take 4 to 6 capsules every morning before breakfast, increasing the amount as needed up to 12 capsules daily (may be taken in divided doses). Take Royal Oil often throughout the day, about 1/2 tsp. as needed. For severe cases take extra pantothenic acid, about 500 mg twice daily.

Allergies

The symptoms of allergies are numerous, in fact, there are hundreds. Allergies are a modern plague. The reason they are a plague is due to the modern way of living. The immune system is weakened by synthetic chemicals. Drugs further weaken it and cause toxic and/or allergic reactions. The food is excessively processed and adulterated, and this increases the risks for the development of food/chemical allergies.

There are thousands of substances that have never before existed on this planet that our bodies must now deal with. These "synthetic" substances, many of which are freely added to commercial foods, are a major cause of allergic reactions. However, natural substances, like citrus, milk, spices, pollen, mold, as well as certain natural-source drugs, such as penicillin, are also a frequent cause of allergic reactions. There is yet another concern: genetically altered foods. The new wave of so called GMO foods is creating havoc with our immune systems. When these foods are consumed, they elicit toxic reactions, which damage the immune cells. The results of a recent study were touted by the genetic engineering industry. Proudly, they proclaimed that engineered potatoes caused "a rise in antibody levels," while the regular potatoes failed to elicit such a response. What they failed to mention was that this is an aberrant reaction. In contrast to the way it is being portrayed by the GMO industry, a rise in antibody levels should not be regarded as a therapeutic response. It is abnormal for a food to induce antibody production. The production of antibodies is a sign that the food is toxic to the organism. The fact is the very basis of allergy testing is the measurement of a rise in antibody levels. The point is the genetically engineered foods are wreaking havoc in the body, not aiding it. A number of illnesses, as well as deaths, have been directly attributed to the consumption of such foods. There is a shockingly high incidence of serious allergic reactions, which are directly attributed to genetically engineered foods. Common symptoms of such allergic reactions include hives, bronchial congestion, swelling in the throat, swelling of the face/eyes, migraines, inflamed joints, and digestive upset. Boycott this corruption by avoiding the intake of commercial foods which are genetically engineered. Eat only organically grown/raised foods.

The adrenal glands play a critical role in protecting the body from allergic reactions. They do so by producing cortisone, which fights inflammation, swelling, and toxicity. Weakened adrenal glands are a major cause of allergic susceptibility. This is why royal jelly is so useful for this condition. It greatly rebuilds these glands, largely because it is an excellent source of pantothenic acid. However, royal jelly offers additional benefits, because it is the number one source or crude steroids, containing some 50 different types, all of which are needed by the adrenal glands. Thus, it is a type of natural cortisone which is free of side effects.

Treatment protocol

Take 2 to 6 capsules of crude fortified royal jelly daily. Once allergic propensities improve take as a maintenance 2 capsules daily. If desired, take a teaspoon of raw honey daily along with 1/2 tsp. of stabilized liquid royal jelly, e.g. Royal Oil. The Royal Oil is different than any other type of royal jelly, as it is emulsified and readily absorbed.

Alzheimer's disease

This has reached epidemic proportions and is the fourth leading cause of death in Western civilization. The disease is rare in primitive societies. What's more, even in the United States it has developed largely since the early 1900's. Cases prior to this were unknown. Dietary indiscretions are a major factor in causing this disease. Usually there is a history of excessive sugar consumption. The diet is high in processed foods of all types, which are loaded with sugar and other noxious ingredients.

To correct the condition it is crucial to curb sugar and processed food intake. Eat fresh organic meat, poultry, fish, vegetables, and fruit. Eliminate alcohol and caffeinated beverages.

Alzheimer's disease is largely a sugar-induced syndrome. Stress also plays a role. The combination of a high amount of stress plus a high sugar diet may precipitate the disease. Refined grains also worsen and/or cause this condition. Eliminate the intake of white flour, white rice, and refined carbohydrates.

Treatment protocol

Take Royal Kick, 4 to 6 capsules every morning. Take an additional 2 to 4 capsules at noon. Take also Royal Oil, 1/2 tsp. twice daily. Strictly avoid the intake of refined sugar as well as white flour and rice. Avoid chocolate and alcoholic beverages.

Anemia

Royal jelly is a blood builder. It has been known for decades that hemoglobin counts increase with royal jelly therapy. This is because it is nutritionally rich, and blood building is nutrient dependent. Everyone is aware that iron is needed for healthy blood. However, protein, in the form of amino acids, is just as important. Royal jelly is an excellent source of this substance. B vitamins, steroids, and trace minerals are also required to regenerate the blood. Anemia is due to the loss of red blood cells. It takes dense nutrition to rebuild cells. With anemia, billions of cells are missing. Thus, the individual needs the most dense sources of nutrition for rebuilding. Royal jelly is one of these dense sources.

Treatment protocol

Royal jelly is potent nourishment, which is direly needed in anemia. This is because anemia is a form of cellular starvation. To rebuild the red cells take large amounts of royal jelly, like 4 capsules twice daily. Once the blood count is normalized take 2 to 4 capsules daily as maintenance. Take Royal Oil, 1/2 tsp. twice or more daily. Also, take crude red grape powder, one of the most potent blood builders known, about one teaspoon twice daily. This is known commercially as Resvitanol powder. Crude grape powder is safe for all ages. To order check health food stores or call 1-800-243-5242. Note: crude red grape powder is completely different than grape seed extract. A number of such extracts contain residues of solvents such as formaldehyde and methyl chloride. Red sour grape is completely free of chemical residues. It is made from the whole grape, that is the skin, seed, and vine. It is a super-dense source of chromium, potassium, crude flavonoids, iron, and vitamin C.

Anorexia

This is defined as total loss of appetite. It occurs most commonly in teenagers, who subsist on an abnormal, that is, nutritionally inferior diet. Royal jelly may prove lifesaving. This is because it aggressively regenerates the appetite, creating a sustained and vigorous desire for food, that is healthy food. Plus, it inhibits the desire for harmful foods, like sweets and starchy snacks. With its rich supply of B vitamins, royal jelly helps stimulate digestion. It regenerates the stomach and intestinal linings. Plus, it helps balance blood sugar to reduce cravings for sugary foods.

Dr. Saenz cites a case of an anorexic teenager considered incurable. This hospitalized patient's only nutrition was via blood transfusions and other IVs. However, incredibly, after the royal jelly treatment the patient completely recovered, gaining back both her weight and appetite.

Treatment protocol

For mild cases take 2 to 4 Royal Kick daily in the morning before breakfast. For severe cases take 6 Royal Kick in the morning along with 1/2 tsp. Royal Oil. Then, take the Royal Oil as needed throughout the day. The crude royal jelly will greatly stimulate and give a natural balance to the appetite, eliminating the anorexia. For additional stimulatory support give edible oil of ginger (in an extra virgin olive oil base), 5 drops under the tongue or in juice/water with each meal.

Anxiety

This condition usually responds immediately to royal jelly. This is largely because royal jelly provides critical nutrients needed by the brain, like pantothenic acid, thiamine, vitamin B-6, riboflavin, biotin, potassium, magnesium, and phosphorus. It is also because royal jelly is one of the richest naturally occurring sources of brain chemicals known as neurotransmitters. The types of neutransmitters in royal jelly are readily digested and absorbed, going directly into the blood. From here, they are carried to the brain, where they act virtually immediately. This illustrates the benefits of sublingual royal jelly, that is the Royal Oil, which, when taken under the tongue, offers rapid absorption into the blood.

Treatment protocol

To balance the mood and prevent mental attacks take the Royal Kick, 2 capsules twice daily. Also, take the crude stabilized royal jelly, 1/2 tsp. under the tongue as often as needed. In addition, eliminate all dietary sources of stimulants. Alcohol and refined sugar should be strictly avoided.

Arthritis

Arthritis is due to a breakdown in the structure of the joint. Joints are held together by connective tissue, which is mostly collagen. In arthritics collagen either wears down, or it becomes diseased, that is inflamed. Royal jelly is a collagen rebuilder. Fortified royal jelly, that is Royal Kick, is a pain fighter. Royal jelly is a natural source of a number of nutrients needed for joint and collagen repair. Collagen is the connective tissue making up cartilage, tendons, and ligaments. The joint surfaces are lined with cartilage. Royal jelly offers the nutrients that the cartilage requires for proper health. In fact, this wondrous substance contains a type of collagen precursor which is rapidly utilized by joints, especially wounded ones. Certainly, royal jelly, as a regenerative substance, is superior to chondroitin sulfate, which is a synthetic supplement.

Treatment protocol

Crude royal jelly, when fortified with pantothenic acid, is a powerful remedy for joint health. Take 4 capsules of fortified royal jelly in the morning and 2 to 4 capsules at noon. Strictly avoid refined sugar consumption. Take also crude royal jelly liquid, 1/2 tsp. twice daily.

Asthma

The asthma epidemic has struck the United States and Canada with a ferocity. As many as one in eight North Americans have it. Incredibly, since the turn of the century the incidence has risen astronomically, the increase being well over 400%.

Modern medicine has completely failed to cure this disease. In fact, since the 1970s the death rate has risen sharply. Recent studies indicate the asthma treatment, that is the use of potent drugs, such as steroids and theophylline, increases the risks for sudden death and may, in fact, largely be the cause for the inordinately high death rate.

Royal jelly is a harmless substance and is highly beneficial for asthmatics. An exception may be the rare case of the asthmatic who is highly allergic to bee stings. In such a case royal jelly may not be usable. However, it can be safety taken in a test dose. Simply take a drop of Royal Oil under the tongue. If a reaction occurs, discontinue use. If it is well tolerated, increase the amount by a drop a day. If using Royal Kick, open a gelatin capsule. Place a sprinkle of the powder under the tongue. If it is well tolerated, increase this amount gradually. Then, begin taking entire capsules by mouth, like one capsule daily for a week, then two capsules the next week, etc., until reaching the optimal amount (4 to 8 capsules daily).

This tactic is only necessary for the ultra-sensitive. The remainder of asthmatics can take the royal jelly more aggressively. However, it is advisable to begin with small amounts, gradually increasing it to tolerance.

Treatment protocol

In addition to the aforementioned advice take Royal Kick, 2 to 6 capsules daily in the a.m. Also, take Royal Oil, 1/2 to 1 tsp. once or twice daily. During an attack take it more often, like 1/2 tsp. every hour.

Attention deficit disorder (ADD)

This is one of the modern world's most disconcerting illnesses, plaguing children as well as adults. It is often represented as a vague disease for which the cause is unknown. The fact is this disorder is due to poor diet. Food allergies also play a role.

Toxicity due to heavy metals, like mercury and lead, often plays a major role.

Nutritional deficiency is a primary cause of ADD. Poor diet leads to nutritional imbalances/deficiencies, and this is the primary cause of ADD. However, ADD is also caused by a breakdown in the hormonal and immune systems. The constant intake of nutrient-defective foods and/or refined sugar weakens the system, leading to a wide range of mental and physical symptoms. Chemicals in food, like food dyes, MSG, sulfites, and NutraSweet, greatly aggravate the problem.

Treatment protocol

Eliminate all sources of refined sugar. Replace refined grains with whole grains. Increase the consumption of nutrient dense foods, like whole milk products, farm fresh fertile eggs, organic meat/poultry, fatty fish, fresh fruit, and fresh vegetables. Children need nutrients. Feed them what they need. Take Royal Kick, about 4 capsules in the morning. Also, take Royal Oil, 1/2 tsp. twice daily. In most instances improvement will be rapid.

Cancer

This is one of the areas where royal jelly may save lives. Because it is a predigested food, it is ideal for cancer victims, since they are always malnourished. Such individuals have diminished energy, so whatever energy they have must be used to eliminated the cancer(s). The digestion of food consumes energy, plus the food may contain chemicals which aggravate the organs. Royal jelly rebuilds health. It is well tolerated even by those with sensitive stomachs. The sublingual type is rapidly absorbed, and nutrients are delivered where they are needed most: directly into the blood so they can be used by the cells.

Research documents that royal jelly contains a number of compounds which strengthen immunity. Certain of these compounds increase the activity of while blood cells, like macrophages, which kill cancer cells. While performed on animals, a Canadian study thoroughly proved that royal jelly is safe for cancer victims, and that, in fact, it greatly increases immune powers. What's more, the length of life was dramatically increased.

In certain cancers the use of hormones is contraindicated. While synthetic hormones can be dangerous, the hormones in royal jelly are non-toxic. Do not be concerned about the naturally occurring hormones in royal jelly. This substance contains a balance of hormones. The hormones are safe for human consumption. The point is royal jelly strengthens the body regardless of the health condition(s). Besides allergic intolerance, there are no contraindications.

Medical doctors often balk at the idea of cancer patients taking an herbal medicine or medicinal food. The average physician has no knowledge regarding the medicinal powers of royal jelly. Yet, royal jelly is 100% safe to take during cancer therapy, plus it is highly effective. Regardless of the type of cancer from which you suffer, take royal jelly: your health will improve as a result.

Treatment protocol

Crude unprocessed royal jelly products, like Royal Kick and Royal Oil, are completely safe for human consumption. With the exception of allergic intolerance, they never cause life-threatening or serious symptoms/illnesses. Take Royal Kick, 4 to 6 capsules daily. Take also Royal Oil under the tongue, 1/2 to 1 tsp. as often as possible. Royal Oil and Royal Kick are completely safe to take in combination with prescription drugs.

Chronic fatigue syndrome

Weak adrenals are major cause of chronic fatigue syndrome. The adrenal glands are a tiny set of glands, about golf ball-sized, which are found on top of each kidney. They produce a variety of hormones, including adrenalin and cortisone. These glands control a wide range of functions, including blood pressure, blood sugar, heart rate, blood flow, protein metabolism, sugar metabolism, and sexual activity. The adrenal glands are the body's coping mechanism. When their function fails, the individual fails to cope normally with everyday stress. Physical and mental energy decline. Chronic fatigue syndrome is one of a number of illnesses that are due to failed adrenal function.

The function of the adrenal glands is dependent upon pantothenic acid, and royal jelly is the best naturally occurring source of this vitamin. Pantothenic acid is needed for adrenal steroid synthesis. A severe lack of pantothenic acid essentially halts steroid synthesis. What's more, royal jelly offers a wide range of natural steroids, which greatly boost adrenal function. Routinely, this condition responds to royal jelly treatment. The secret is to determine the correct dosage for the individual. The rule is when in doubt increase the amount until results are achieved.

Treatment protocol

Take 4 to 12 capsules of crude fortified royal jelly in the morning before breakfast. Take also Royal Oil, a half teaspoon or more under the tongue as often as needed. Use sea salt in cooking. For more information regarding the role of salt in chronic fatigue syndrome see Dr. Ingram's books *Lifesaving Cures* and *SuperMarket Remedies*.

Crohn's disease

This is one of the most devastating of all illnesses. Unchecked, it leads to destruction of the small intestine and colon, ultimately resulting in surgical removal. The disease may spread throughout the gut, causing extensive damage and/or disability. Death may occur.

Crohn's disease is a dietary illness. This condition is unknown in primitive societies, that is in regions wherein people consume unprocessed food. The typical American diet is a major cause of disease, and Crohn's disease is one of hundreds of diet-induced syndromes. Foods to strictly avoid include refined sugar, processed flour products, nitrated meats, refined vegetable oils, and hydrogenated oils. Read labels, and be sure to avoid these substances. Alcoholic beverages, as well as chocolate, also aggravate the illness.

Individuals with Crohn's disease invariably suffer from weakened adrenal glands. If the adrenal glands are strengthened, the Crohn's disease improves. This illustrates the value of crude royal jelly, since it is perhaps the most potent adrenal gland tonic known.

Treatment protocol
Take Royal Kick, 4 to 6 capsules every morning. If necessary, take another 2 to 4 capsules at noon. Also, take stabilized liquid royal jelly, 1/2 tsp. as often as needed.

Cold sores

This is due to a herpes infection of the nerves. The virus may live deep inside the nerves, where it hides from the immune system. The herpes exits the nerves, usually about the lips. This leads to the characteristic oral lesions. Stress, drug therapy, chemotherapy, radiation treatments, and chocolate provoke attacks. Cortisone is one of the most aggressive drugs in precipitating attacks.

Royal jelly blocks the toxic effects of stress. Plus, it supplies anti-viral and antiinflammatory substances. It is a reliable remedy for minimizing and/or reversing these lesions.

Treatment protocol

To eradicate the lesion(s) take 2 or more capsules of fortified royal jelly powder as often as is necessary. Make a paste with raw honey and Royal Oil; apply topically.

Depression

Royal jelly usually dramatically assists this condition. Certainly, lifestyle issues must also be addressed. Dietary indiscretions are a major cause of depression. There are also serious medical causes, yet, in most instances there is a major nutritional/dietary role. Frequently, the individual is addicted to sweets, chocolate, pastries, cookies, starch (bread, rolls, potatoes, etc.). Stress is also a major cause, but it does so by depleting the body of critical substances, like vitamins, minerals, and hormones. Alcohol consumption is also a major factor. Like sugar, alcohol destroys a wide range of nutrients direly needed by the brain. Plus, it is directly toxic to brain cells. A mere ounce or two of hard liquor destroys as many as a million brain cells.

For chronic depression royal jelly is a safe and effective supplement. Use crude raw royal jelly to boost mental strength and replenish the deficits. It provides nutrients rarely found elsewhere: neurotransmitters, such as acetylcholine, and genetic material, that is RNA and DNA. The latter is highly valuable for regenerating nerve function.

Treatment protocol

There should be a quick response to royal jelly treatment. Take Royal Kick, three to four capsules twice daily. Use the Royal Oil often, like 1/2 tsp. three or more times daily. Take it repeatedly until results are obtained. Be sure to eliminate from the diet refined foods, sugar, wheat, corn, and alcohol. Also, take a water-soluble extract of wild rosemary, i.e. the Juice of Rosemary, one ounce twice daily in juice or in hot water as a tea.

Diabetes

In the Western world diabetes has reached epidemic proportions. Unfortunately, modern medicine has offered no means of curing it. Symptoms are controlled by drugs and insulin injections. However, the disease usually progresses, causing disability, disfigurement, and/or premature death.

This is a diet induced disease. There is no need to spend billions of dollars searching for some supposedly elusive "diabetic gene." The cause is more obvious: what we eat and/or what we fail to eat. Refined sugar consumption is directly related to the onset of diabetes. So is the consumption of white flour and white rice. In societies wherein sugar consumption is limited diabetes is rare.

Royal jelly is of immense value for diabetics. This is largely because of its positive actions on the adrenal glands. The latter are   severely weakened in diabetics. The Royal Oil is of particular value, because it contains other useful substances such as crude pumpkinseed oil and spice antioxidants. Spice extracts have been shown to act as natural blood sugar lowering agents. Crude pumpkinseed oil contains linoleic acid, which aids in fat metabolism and helps prevent the accumulation of fat in the arteries.

The regular use of royal jelly reduces sugar cravings. It also increases stress tolerance, plus it boosts immunity.

Treatment protocol

Take crude royal jelly powder (fortified), 4 to 6 capsules every morning. Also, take liquid stabilized royal jelly (Royal Oil), 1/2 to 1 tsp. twice daily. To achieve optimal results be consistent. For difficult cases take higher amounts. For diabetic wounds mix Royal Oil in raw honey, and apply it on the wound. Cover and leave for at least 24 hours, then repeat as needed. Strictly avoid the intake of refined sugar, white flour products, white rice, caffeine, and alcohol. Crude sources of B vitamins are also helpful; diabetics are severely deficient in this category of nutrients. The B vitamins are needed for sugar metabolism. As a source of crude niacin and thiamine take Nutri-Sense, three tablespoons once or twice daily. This provides high amounts of natural thiamine, niacin, biotin, and lesser but important amounts of pantothenic acid. Marmite is another crude extract. This is a yeast extract and is well tolerated by the majority of individuals; take one teaspoon twice daily. Marmite is rich in all of the major B vitamins.

Oregulin is a medicinal spice extract specifically formulated for diabetics. This natural formula has been proven by preliminary scientific studies to support the blood sugar mechanism. One study determined that it also helped normalize blood pressure. Oregulin is being successfully used by hundreds of diabetics. For more information or to order Oregulin see the Web site Oregulin.com or call 1-800-243-5242.

Eczema

This disconcerting disorder is caused by a variety of factors. Poor diet greatly increases the risks. The fact is eczema is rare in societies subsisting on natural or unprocessed foods. The foods to avoid include refined sugar, adulterated fats, chocolate, and processed grains. Food allergies may aggravate eczema. However, the major factor appears to be a breakdown of the immune system. This breakdown leads to infection within the body, which may spread to the skin. Researchers at the University of Tennessee discovered that eczematous lesions are infected, usually by fungi but also by bacteria, particularly staph or strep. Apparently, the fungi arise from within the body and eventually attack and feed off the skin.

The good news is that the fungi may be killed. Drugs are somewhat effective. However, safer therapies include oil of oregano, cinnamon extracts, and oil of bay leaf. One study by Georgetown University determined that a special type of oil of oregano, known as P73 Oreganol, completely destroyed all fungi against which it was tested.

Royal jelly is also an antimicrobial agent. Plus, it greatly enhances skin health. With its rich content of hydroxy fatty acids, it acidifies the skin, strengthening its immune system so that germs cannot invade. It also directly nourishes the skin, creating healthy cells which are resistant to disease. Royal jelly contains a wide range of skin nourishing nutrients, including riboflavin, pantothenic acid, niacin, pyridoxine, and vitamins C, A, and E. Its hormones are also helpful in the healing of damaged skin, since they act as a natural type of cortisone.

Treatment protocol

Take crude royal jelly, about 4 to 6 capsules daily. Also, take the liquid stabilized type, 1/2 tsp. twice daily. Oreganol (P73) is a type of wild oregano, which has been proven to kill fungi. Take one or two capsules of Oreganol twice daily.

Endometriosis

In this debilitating condition menstrual fluid regurgitates from the uterus against gravity into the fallopian tubes, on the ovaries, and into the abdomen. This leads to severe inflammation and, therefore, pain. The point is the menstrual fluids are supposed to flow forward not backward.

The condition may be complicated and/or caused by infection, particularly yeast infections. In this instance the yeasts must be eliminated to achieve a cure.

Endometriosis may be due in part to nutritional deficiency, which leads to a weakening in the function of the female organs. Thus, in order for the condition to be resolved the female organs must be strengthened, both nutritionally and hormonally. Royal jelly is the ideal nutritional/hormonal tonic for the female glands. By strengthening the health of the cells of the uterus, ovaries, and fallopian tubes the body is more resistant to developing such an aberrant condition.

Treatment protocol

Georgetown University proved that yeasts, particularly the notoriously difficult to kill Candida albicans, are eradicated by oil of wild oregano. Using the P73 wild Mediterranean type (e.g. Oreganol™), they completely destroyed this fungus in experimental animals. No trace of the fungus remained. Royal Oil is a potent type of stabilized crude royal jelly; take 1/2 to 1 tsp. twice daily. Take also Royal Kick, 4 to 6 capsules every morning before breakfast. Avoid sexual intercourse during menses.

Failure to thrive

Millions of children suffer all over the globe from growth failure.

In America this is particularly tragic, because remedies are available to cure this dilemma. Royal jelly is one of the most potent growth enhancers known. Because of its diverse array of potent hormones and proteins, it aids the growth of any organ, even the bones and muscles.

Treatment protocol

Regardless of the age take as much royal jelly as is necessary to boost growth. Begin with 2 capsules and 1/2 tsp., and increase these amounts as needed. Eliminate from the diet processed foods. Increase the intake of protein-rich foods, like fresh organic red meat, organ meats, poultry, fish, whole milk products, eggs, nuts, beans, and seeds.

Fibromyalgia

No one seems to know what causes this condition, but the latest evidence points to immune breakdown due to infection, the likely culprits being molds and mycoplasma. Food allergies may also play a role. In particular, the major issue is allergic intolerance to grains. Certainly, severe stress aggravates it. Thus, individuals with fibromyalgia may also suffer from adrenal weakness. Royal jelly rebuilds the immune and adrenal systems, and in this respect it may reverse many of the symptoms of this disease.

Treatment protocol

Take large amounts of the fortified/stabilized royal jelly, like 6 to 8 capsules daily. Also, take Royal Oil, one tsp. twice daily. As a means of eradicating persistent germs take also Oreganol gelcaps, one or more twice daily.

Fungal infections

Infections by fungi affect a huge percentage of North Americans. As many as 50% of Americans suffer from some sort of fungal infection.

Fungi may infect any organ or tissue in the body. However, they have a particular propensity for the mucous membranes, such as the membranes of the mouth, sinuses, bronchial tree, vagina, and urethra. They also readily attack the skin and scalp.

Fungal infections signal a breakdown in the endocrine system. When the endocrine glands are weak, fungi easily invade the body. This is why royal jelly is so valuable. It regenerates the endocrine glands, allowing the body to eradicate the fungal infestation. In other words, unless the endocrine dysfunction is resolved, the fungal infection will often fail to be cured.

Treatment protocol

Take on a routine basis 4 to 6 Royal Kick daily. Take also Royal Oil, 1/2 tsp. twice daily. It may take weeks or months to regenerate the endocrine glands, but it will be worth the effort. Take also Oreganol gelcaps, one twice daily.

Hair loss and graying of the hair

Royal jelly has been long known as a potent remedy for hair problems. It has reversed both hair loss and graying of the hair. It is particularly valuable for reversing hair loss due to toxic chemical exposure or glandular imbalances. However, the results are not universal. Yet, in severe cases there is usually at least some benefit. Royal jelly is the top source of pantothenic acid, a nutrient proven to reverse graying of the hair.

Treatment protocol

Take large amounts of the fortified/stabilized royal jelly, like 6 to 8 capsules daily. Also, take Royal Oil, 1/2 tsp. twice daily. Eliminate the consumption of refined sugar and alcohol. Use an herbal based fragrance-free shampoo. Also, use Scalp Clenz, an essential oil-based formula for boosting hair/scalp health. Simply rub Scalp Clenz into the scalp once daily.

Hepatitis

Defined as inflammation of the liver, hepatitis is usually caused by infection, although chemical toxicity may also be a culprit. Viruses are the main infectious agent, although parasites, like amoebas and flukes, are an important secondary cause. Alcohol consumption is the primary cause of chemical hepatitis.

Royal jelly is a supportive therapy for this condition. In contrast to drugs it is completely safe to take for liver disease and will usually aid in liver cell regeneration. Thus, royal jelly may be helpful in normalizing elevated liver enzyme levels.

Treatment protocol

Sugar and alcohol must be eliminated. Take crude royal jelly fortified with pantothenic acid, i.e. Royal Kick, 4 to 6 capsules daily. Take also the liquid type under the tongue, about 1/2 tsp. twice daily. Be sure to avoid the intake of alcoholic beverages, including wine. Limit refined sugar consumption. Carefully read all labels; foods containing synthetic chemicals should not be consumed. Avoid the use of chemical-based cleaners. A recent study found that housekeepers who use chemicals in the home are at a heightened risk for developing chemical hepatitis.

Immune deficiency

This is associated with protein deficiency, specifically a deficiency of immunoglobulins as well as albumin. Royal jelly contains both of these substances. Plus, it contains a plethora of amino acids, which are needed for the formation of immunglobulins as well as white blood cells. Individuals with low white counts should rely upon royal jelly for cellular regeneration. The regular intake will rapidly lead to an improvement in white blood cell counts.

Treatment protocol

Take large amounts of the fortified/stabilized royal jelly, like 6 to 12 capsules daily. Also, take Royal Oil, 1 tsp. two or three times daily.

Impotence

This is one of the most responsive conditions to royal jelly treatment. Royal jelly is one of the few natural sources of sex steroids. It contains small amounts of testosterone, which helps rejuvenate sexual powers. It also contains pantothenic acid, which is needed by the adrenals and testes for testosterone synthesis.

Physical causes appear to play the primary role in causing this condition. Excessive consumption of alcohol weakens the sex glands. So does the excessive intake of caffeinated beverages. Poor circulation, that is hardening of the arteries and/or coronary artery disease, also plays a role. Vitamins and minerals needed to maintain potency include pantothenic acid, folic acid, choline, inositol, vitamin B-12, vitamin C, vitamin E, vitamin A, magnesium, selenium, and zinc. Royal jelly contains all of these nutrients.

Treatment protocol

Take large amounts of the fortified/stabilized royal jelly, like 6 to 8 capsules daily. Also, take Royal Oil, 1/2 to 1 tsp. twice daily. When results are achieved, reduce the amount to 2 to 4 capsules twice daily as a maintenance.

Infertility

This condition is often due to hormone deficiency. This is why royal jelly is so effective. It supplies a dense amount of natural hormones of the type which are completely safe for human consumption. The royal jelly hormones are certainly safer than fertility drugs. The latter may cause a wide range of side effects, including liver, skin, hormonal, and kidney disorders. In contrast, there is not even one incident of harm to the body from the intake of the hormones of royal jelly.

Treatment protocol

Take large amounts of the fortified/stabilized royal jelly, like 6 to 8 capsules daily. Also, take Royal Oil, 1/2 to 1 tsp. twice daily. A weakened thyroid gland leads to infertility. ThyroKelp is a completely natural supplement specifically designed for improving thyroid gland function. Its active ingredient is a rare form of unprocessed northern oceanic kelp, tested to be free of contaminants. Kelp harvested from oceans near industrialized regions is notoriously contaminated.

Ideally, use the royal jelly therapy to boost the adrenal glands, while using the ThyroKelp to bolster thyroid function. For mild cases of weak thyroid function take four to six capsules daily. For more severe cases take up to twelve capsules daily. ThyroKelp is completely non-toxic, that is it is safe to take with any medication.

Insomnia

This condition often quickly responds to royal jelly. It is a debacle for an ill person to have insomnia. This is because if an individual is ill, he/she must get his/her sleep to recover from the illness. Yet, insomnia is a symptom of dozens of illnesses. For the tissues to regenerate sleep must be achieved. The lack of sleep aggravates and/or perpetuates the illness. Thus, it is necessary to sleep soundly, but not by taking mind altering medications. Sleep is necessary for the normal rejuvenating/healing processes. Harsh medications disrupt brain chemistry, which further interferes with healing. A natural sleep must be induced, that is the nervous system must be put into balance so that the body can relax. This is precisely what royal jelly achieves.

Treatment protocol

Take royal jelly in the morning, about 4 capsules before or with breakfast. If agitated at night, before retiring eat a salty snack and take one or two Royal Kick, or take Royal Oil, 1/2 tsp. under the tongue. For difficult cases try Herbal Zeeez, an all natural herbal sleep-inducing tonic. Herbal Zeeez is made from wild herbs with natural and non-toxic relaxation and sedative actions. It helps induce a natural and solid sleep. Take 5 to 10 drops under the tongue before retiring. This is a highly effective sleep tonic; it works quickly and safely. To order call 1-800-243-5242.

Irritable Bowel Syndrome

Royal jelly is of immense value for irritable/spastic colon. It is a delicate yet effective digestive aid, which is sorely needed in this condition. It helps relax the over-worked colonic nerves and eases spastic muscles. Plus, it helps rebuild the natural tone of the colon, so it is able to heal and regenerate. The regular intake of royal jelly balances the nervous system, which greatly aids in the healing of this condition.

Treatment protocol

To ease the spasms and heal damaged tissue take Royal Kick, 4 to 6 capsules every morning with breakfast. Take an additional 1 or 2 capsules with meals. Take also Royal Oil, 1/2 to 1 tsp. twice daily. Avoid alcohol, refined sugar, white flour, coffee, and corn.

Jet lag

The effects of crude royal jelly in reversing jet lag are impressive. I rarely get jet lag, as long as I take the Royal Kick as well as the Royal Oil. The latter is ideal for consuming while in the air. Simply squirt the Royal Oil under the tongue, several squirts during the flight. For a long flight I often consume an entire bottle of Royal Oil, and this routinely prevents jet lag.

Malnourished (sickly) kids

Children in Western countries are malnourished. The obesity epidemic in these children is one example. Acne, high cholesterol, skin disorders, weakened immunity, asthma, greasy hair, fatigue, joint pain, poor posture, short stature, weak muscles, and attention deficit are all examples of malnourishment.

The most serious sign of malnourishment is failure to grow or thrive. This is the ideal usage for royal jelly. It provides such potent nourishment that it can rapidly reverse malnourishment in any child or, for that matter, adults as well. It is readily absorbed and quickly utilized, far faster and more efficiently than any other food or supplement. It is a must for the malnourished.

Treatment protocol

The ideal type to take is the stabilized chocolate-like creamy liquid (i.e. the Royal Oil), as many squirts as is necessary to achieve the desired effect. The crude liquid is non-toxic, so it can be taken in unlimited amounts. This stabilized royal jelly oil is rich in essential fatty acids, because, in addition to the royal jelly it contains cold pressed pumpkinseed oil. The pumpkinseed oil is an excellent source of natural hormones, essential fatty acids, and fat soluble vitamins. It provides gamma tocopherol, which is lacking in royal jelly. Thus, the stabilized fortified royal jelly is superior to the plain creamy-colored type found in health food stores. This is because it contains additional nutrients found in limited supplies in the plain type. Plus, it is transportable, meaning there is no need for refrigeration. It actually tastes good, which is another benefit. Other raw royal jellys have a very bitter taste and, therefore, are more difficult to consume. Also, take stabilized royal jelly powder, about 2 capsules or more daily. For children open the capsules, and add the powder to cereals or shakes.

Menopausal syndrome

This is known as the "change of life." Yet, there is no need to undergo such a dramatic change. In other words, with the proper treatment, all of the symptoms may be avoided. This is a time when hormone levels decline, so by building up the hormone levels the symptoms can be prevented or eradicated.

Royal jelly is the ideal nutritional tonic for this syndrome. This is because it enriches the function of the female hormonal glands.

Its potent natural steroids help aggressively correct glandular imbalances. Yet, it provides these benefits without side effects. Synthetic estrogens pollute our bodies and the environment. Recently, it was discovered that tap water is contaminated with the residues of estrogenic drugs. A number of bizarre syndromes, including premature puberty in girls and breast development in men, are correlated with estrogen pollution. The regular use of royal jelly naturally boosts hormone levels. If you take it regularly, you may be able to completely avoid the change.

Treatment protocol

Take Royal Kick, 4 to 6 capsules every morning. If hot flashes occur, take one or two capsules as often as needed until the symptoms abate. Use also the stabilized liquid royal jelly, about 1/2 tsp. twice daily or as often as needed.

Menstrual cramps

This is where royal jelly is exceptionally powerful. It assists virtually every menstrual-related complaint. This is because it dramatically boosts the body's hormone stores, reducing the stress load on the female organs. In other words, royal jelly supplies female hormones, so the organs don't have to work as hard to produce them.

Royal jelly also boosts adrenal function, and a defect in these glands is tied to menstrual difficulty. Weak adrenal glands are a major cause of menstrual pain/cramps. The adrenal glands produce cortisone, which fights stress and inflammation. When these glands are weakened as a result of stress or poor diet, they fail to produce sufficient cortisone. The result is weakness of a variety of organ systems, including the menstrual response.

Royal jelly greatly strengthens the adrenal glands. It also acts directly upon the female organs, boosting the normal function of the ovaries and uterus. Menstrual discomfort may also be due to infection, notably yeast infection by the notorious Candida albicans.

Treatment protocol

Chocolate and coffee must be avoided. Also, eliminate from the diet refined sugar. Take Royal Kick, about 2 to 4 capsules every morning. If cramps strike, take another one or two capsules as often as needed. Use also the stabilized liquid royal jelly, about 1/2 tsp. twice daily.

Migraine headaches

This is one of the most debilitating of all illnesses. Migraines are largely caused by food allergy, but they may also be caused by infections and toxic chemicals. Blood sugar imbalances may also lead to migraines.

Migraineurs often suffer from weak adrenal glands. These glands produce steroid hormones, for instance, cortisone. The steroid hormones are the body's pain fighters, plus they are needed for regulating blood sugar levels. When steroid hormones are depleted, migraines may result. The adrenal steroids control blood sugar levels, and a deficiency of them results in low blood sugar. A drop in blood sugar means that the brain fails to get the glucose it needs, and this can precipitate a migraine.

Royal jelly helps normalize adrenal function. This is why it is so valuable for reversing migraines. The mechanism of action is that it nourishes the glands, providing them with critical vitamins needed for adrenal steroid synthesis as well as providing the steroids themselves. It also supplies neurotransmitters, which help regenerate brain cells that are weakened by prolonged pain or the over-use of brain-altering medications.

Treatment protocol

For prevention take fortified royal jelly (Royal Kick), 2 to 4 capsules daily. If a migraine strikes, take 1 or 2 capsules of crude royal jelly every hour. Take stabilized liquid royal jelly, that is Royal Oil, under the tongue as often as needed.

Neurodermatitis

Royal jelly is particularly valuable for this skin condition. In fact, this condition responds so thoroughly that it is as if it is due to a "royal jelly deficiency." As the name implies in neurodermatitis the nervous system is in a dysfunctional state. Royal jelly provides potent nutrition to this system, helping to induce a state of balance. Plus, it nourishes the skin, allowing the damaged cells to heal.

Treatment protocol

Take stabilized royal jelly liquid under the tongue, 1/2 tsp. twice daily. Also, take fortified royal jelly powder (e. g. Royal Kick), 4 capsules every morning.

Ovarian cysts

This is one of the most common causes of severe and or sudden abdominal pain. It is particularly common in teenagers and young adults. Cysts are also common in obese women, who frequently suffer from ovarian disorders. Repeated ovarian cysts warn of hypothyroidism.

Poor diet may lead to ovarian cysts. Certain vitamins are needed to maintain ovarian health. Chief among them are vitamins A, C, and E plus the B-complex, particularly folic and pantothenic acid. The essential fatty acids are also usually deficient. Royal jelly provides a healthy balance of all of these nutrients.

Treatment protocol

To prevent this disorder take two Royal Kick, which is fortified with pantothenic acid, daily. In the event of an attack take two to four Royal Kick every four to six hours. Also, take Royal Oil under the tongue once or twice daily. Folic acid is also needed; take one milligram daily. Eat fatty fish, like salmon, mackerel, albacore tuna, and halibut, on a regular basis.

Pancreatitis

This condition is due to inflammation of the pancreas. The cause of the inflammation is usually infection, although excessive alcohol intake is also a prominent factor. Toxic chemicals readily damage the pancreas and may induce the condition. James F. Balch, M. D., notes that royal jelly has been shown to be effective against pancreatitis. This is largely because of the fact that royal jelly is predigested. Thus, its intake fails to stress the pancreas.

Treatment protocol

Take crude stabilized royal jelly, about 1 tsp. under the tongue twice daily. Avoid solid food, sipping only on beef or chicken broth. Curtail alcohol consumption.

Panic attacks

In most instances panic attacks respond quickly to royal jelly. This is partially because of royal jelly's content of the anti-stress vitamin, pantothenic acid. It is also because royal jelly helps calm the nerves, since it provides nourishment in the form of the B complex, calming minerals, and the all-important nerve transmission chemical: acetylcholine.

Panic attacks are a classic symptom of adrenal insufficiency. The adrenal glands are the organ responsible for the ability to cope. What would normally be a minor event is an arduous or frightening one for the adrenally insufficient.

Treatment protocol
Take 4 to 6 capsules of fortified royal jelly in the morning. Use the stabilized crude royal jelly, 1/2 tsp. or more as often as needed. Reduce the intake of refined sugar.

Parkinson's disease

In this disease the entire nervous system degenerates, although the greatest brunt of the damage is sustained by the brain. Researchers have discovered that a certain portion of the brain, known as the substantia nigra, degenerates. The most likely cause is a virus, however, recent evidence implicates pesticide and herbicide toxicity. These ubiquitous chemicals are fat soluble, and, thus, they readily enter the fatty brain. There they wreak havoc, weakening and destroying nerve cells. This leaves the brain cells vulnerable to invasion by a host of germs, including fungi and viruses. In particular, the herpes virus has been found in the nerve tissue and brains of victims of neurological diseases.

A number of researchers have proven that there is a link between pesticide and herbicide exposure and Parkinson's disease. Pesticides/herbicides deplete critical nutrients, like vitamins B-1, B-3, B-6, and B-12. Interestingly, all of the aforementioned nutrients are provided by royal jelly. There is another reason royal jelly may help this condition: hormone dysfunction. Pesticides interfere with hormone metabolism.

Royal jelly provides natural hormones direly needed by the brain. The hormones can then be used by the brain cells for stimulating repair—perhaps regeneration. This may explain why physicians report that certain individuals with Parkinson's disease have improved vastly from royal jelly therapy. Whatever the mechanism, the regenerative powers of royal jelly make it the supplement of choice for this devastating condition.

Treatment protocol

Take Royal Kick fortified royal jelly, 4 capsules twice daily. Take also Royal Oil, 1 tsp. twice daily. Also, drink Essence of Orange Blossom (a tea/tonic for aiding brain cell balance); simply add two or three tablespoons of the Essence in a cup of hot water; drink two or three cups daily. To order this lovely tasting and mind-supporting tonic call 1-800-243-5242.

PMS

PMS, or premenstrual tension, afflicts tens of millions of North American women. Interestingly, this condition is relatively rare in primitive regions, where the diet is largely devoid of processed foods. Thus, there is a significant dietary cause of this illness. In particular, the consumption of refined sugar, as well as foods containing caffeine, appears to aggravate it.

For millions of women the menstrual period is a painful burden. Yet, it is an unnecessary one. This is because premenstrual symptoms can largely be reversed by building the body up nutritionally, eliminating processed foods, and consuming nutrient dense ones. To reverse these symptoms, eat primarily fresh organic meat, fresh vegetables, fresh fruit, nuts, seeds, and whole grains. This diet alone will largely resolve the condition.

Royal jelly is the most potent of all types of nutritional support for the female glands. It provides the nutrients and hormones needed to keep these glands in optimal health.

Treatment protocol

Take the fortified crude royal jelly, 4 to 6 capsules every morning. Also, take Royal Oil, 1/2 tsp. or more under the tongue as often as needed. Strictly avoid the intake of chocolate, refined sugar, tea, and coffee.

Psoriasis

This is one of the greatest plagues of modern civilization. Psoriasis afflicts tens of millions of North Americans. It particularly strikes people of European descent. It is directly related to the modern diet. The fact is this disease is almost exclusively found in Western civilizations. What these civilizations have in common is a diet consisting largely of processed and adulterated foods.

A high consumption of refined sugars and starches is a part of the cause. Other factors include severe stress and anxiety, which weaken the immune system. The repeated use of pharmaceutical drugs, particularly antibiotics and cortisone, may also instigate it.

Psoriasis appears to always be due to a malfunction of the immune system. When the immune system falters, the body is invaded by fungi as well as toxic bacteria, like staph and strep. The germs colonize within the intestines and other organs. Eventually, they enter the blood and, seeking food, invade the skin, where nourishment is rich.

The original research regarding the role of fungi in psoriasis was performed at the University of Tennessee. There, physicians determined that psoriasis plaques were contaminated with fungi as well as bacteria. The prescribed therapy was topical antifungal and antibacterial agents. When the germs were killed, the psoriasis disappeared. However, relapses were common.

Topical therapies have been the mainstay of modern medicine. Yet, these therapies fail to address a crucial factor: that the germs largely arise from within the tissues. Thus, a permanent result is largely dependent upon improving internal health and destroying germ pockets within the body.

Treatment protocol

Use a natural antiseptic to kill the fungi. Oreganol is ideal. This is the oil of oregano researched with proven results at Georgetown University (P73 wild high mountain oregano). Take 5 or more drops twice daily under the tongue. Take sublingual royal jelly, 10 to 20 drops twice daily. Take also stabilized/fortified royal jelly, that is Royal Kick, 4 capsules twice daily on an empty stomach.

Radiation damage

The body is quickly damaged by radiation. There are numerous sources of tissue damaging radiation. These sources include computers, cell phones, microwave ovens/dishes, sunlight, radioactive medical tests, x-rays, radiation therapy, televisions, nuclear/food irradiation plants, and numerous others.

Radiation damages cells by oxidizing them. This leads to massive inflammation and, ultimately, cell death. Thus, antioxidants may block the damage. Royal jelly contains dozens of natural antioxidants, including vitamin A, vitamin E, pantothenic acid, hydroxy acids, sterols, and vitamin C. Other antioxidant-rich substances which help protect the body against radiation include grape extracts, turmeric, rosemary, sage, cloves, and oregano.

As radiation causes massive inflammation it is important to realize that royal jelly contains an antidote: antiinflammatory steroids. Its rich content of steroids reduces inflammation. Yet, royal jelly's greatest value is because of yet another group of compounds: nucleic acids. Radiation is highly toxic to the cells' nuclei (the plural of nucleus). In fact, this is how radiation causes cell death, that is by destroying the nucleus. RNA and DNA are needed to quickly repair the damage. Royal jelly is the richest natural source of RNA and DNA known.

Treatment protocol

Certain vitamins block or reverse radiation damage. Pantothenic acid, the key vitamin in royal jelly, is perhaps the most important. Other vitamins which reverse radiation poisoning include riboflavin, folic acid, vitamin B-12, vitamin A, beta carotene, and vitamin C. Selenium is also crucial for protecting cells against radiation. Take Royal Kick, 4 to 6 capsules in the morning. Also, take Royal Oil, 1/2 to 1 tsp. twice daily. A special antioxidant and anti-radiation formula is available which encapsulates the critical anti-radiation vitamins and minerals. Called Nuke Protect™, this formula is specific for reversing severe radiation toxicity. However, it can also be taken to block the ill effects of low level radiation such as exposure from cellular phones, high tension power lines, or solar rays. Take 2 or more capsule daily.

Stomach ulcers

Royal jelly aids healing. It is well tolerated by those with sensitive digestion or weakened tissues. Plus, it is easily digested even by the most weakened system. This is why it is ideal in stomach ulcers. Royal jelly provides micro-doses of naturally occurring pantothenic acid, the most powerful tissue healing vitamin known.

Treatment protocol

To heal the digestive lining take Royal Kick, 2 to 4 capsules twice daily. Also, take stabilized royal jelly under the tongue, 10 drops three times daily.

Sugar addiction

Millions of individuals are thoroughly addicted to sugar. The high sugar intake damages health, leading to a wide range of diseases, including hypoglycemia, diabetes, fungal infections, chronic fatigue syndrome, adrenal weakness, arthritis, kidney disorders, mental diseases, and heart disease. The diabetic epidemic is directly caused by high sugar intake. Cancer of the intestines also appears to be related to excessive sugar intake, as is Alzheimer's disease.

Sugar addictions may be difficult to resolve. This is why royal jelly is so valuable. It induces regeneration in the glands, particularly the adrenal glands, and this results in a reduction in the cravings. Eventually, the unbridled desire for sugar is diminished and, thus, the addiction can be broken.

Treatment protocol.

Take Royal Kick, 4 capsules every morning upon arising and another capsule or two whenever sugar cravings strike. Also, take the Royal Oil under the tongue, a half to one teaspoon as often as needed. This royal jelly therapy works faster by increasing the consumption of natural-source B vitamins. Consume Nutri-Sense, about three tablespoons twice daily in juice or water. Add it to whole grain cereal. Its rich content of natural thiamine and niacin help diminish sugar cravings. Also, consume Marmite yeast extract, about one teaspoon twice daily.

Sun damage (of the skin)

Solar rays are one of the most powerful oxidizing agents known. It is believed that solar damage of the skin is irreversible. However, royal jelly aids in skin regeneration. This action is largely the result of its ability to thoroughly nourish skin cells. Plus, royal jelly contains a number of compounds, such as DNA and RNA, which induce cellular regeneration. The steroid hormones it contains are ideal for naturally reducing inflammation. Thus, it is the ideal treatment for this condition. Usually, both internal and external use are required.

Treatment protocol
Use a topical royal jelly cream, applying as often as necessary. Also, take stabilized royal jelly under the tongue, 1/2 to 1 tsp. twice daily.

Tuberculosis

This dreaded infection is again becoming a global epidemic. As many as one in three individuals globally have it. It may strike suddenly and, currently, virtually everyone is vulnerable to its development. However, individuals who are most vulnerable include children, the elderly, people on chemotherapy, or individuals with weakened immune systems. In addition, AIDS victims have a high rate of infection, as do the health care workers who treat them.

TB is a fulminant epidemic. Within the next 20 years perhaps as many as one in three individuals will develop active infections. Tuberculosis patients often suffer from malnourishment, which further weakens their already compromised immune systems. This is why royal jelly is so valuable. It nourishes all cells, giving the body the greatest potential for resisting and overcoming debilitating infections. Plus, it contains antibacterial compounds which assist the immune cells in eradicating germs.

Treatment protocol

Take large quantities, like 4 capsules of stabilized royal jelly (e.g. Royal Kick), three times a day. Take under the tongue Royal Oil, 1/2 to 1 tsp. twice daily.

Viral infections

When viruses attack the body, they weaken it. This ability to incapacitate the cells is how they invade. A strong system is relatively immune to viruses. Royal jelly helps reverse the weakness induced by viruses. Plus, it helps keep the cells strong, so they are more resistant to viral invasion. Thus, its major value is in prevention. The regular intake of royal jelly reduces the incidence of viral infections. Royal jelly also contains potent antiviral compounds, so it is also of value to take during a viral attack.

Treatment protocol

To prevent viral attack take 2 to 4 capsules of stabilized royal jelly once or twice daily. Also, take Royal Oil,1/2 tsp. once or twice daily. To reverse an attack take 4 capsules of stabilized royal jelly several times daily along with several drops of Royal Oil as many times daily as possible. This treatment should help reduce the severity of the attack.

Wound healing

It was Paavo Ariola, N.D., world renowned naturopath, who described how royal jelly speeds the healing of wounds, reducing healing time by up to 50%. The effect is largely due to its pantothenic acid content, a vitamin well respected for its ability to bolster wound healing. However, royal jelly's rich content of steroids accounts for its wound healing powers, since the steroids also assist healing by reducing inflammation and swelling. Plus, royal jelly contains antibacterial hydroxy acids, which help the body in the destruction of noxious germs, like E. coli, strep, and staph. Dr. Ariola notes that royal jelly has proven antibacterial actions against these germs.

Treatment protocol

Add royal jelly to honey; apply on the wound. Take liquid stabilized royal jelly under the tongue, 1/2 to 1 tsp. twice daily. For severe wounds take also Royal Kick, 3 to 4 capsules twice daily. Be persistent; it takes time to regenerate the tissue, especially if the wounds are severe or multiple. Royal jelly provides the critical nutrients it needs to induce healing

Chapter 4

Clinical Observations

Royal jelly has been used by the human race for thousands of years. It was prescribed as a medicine as well as cosmetic aid. This substance was highly valued in various ancient civilizations, because it produced measurable results. It is reasonable to presume that if it was of such immense value for past civilizations it would be equally if not more valuable today. Even so, for many individuals what the ancients did seems superfluous. The desire is for current data. What follows is actual modern data: human case histories, scientific studies on humans, and scientific studies on animals.

A number of scientists and physicians have tested royal jelly on humans and animals. A wide range of results have been observed. The results are positive and rarely if ever negative. Experiments have been performed on a wide range of creatures, including insects, pigs, mice, rats, chickens, and, yes, humans, including premature babies and infants. Many of the human studies have been performed in Europe and the Orient, where people greatly believe in the powers of royal jelly and routinely use it.

In Argentina researchers monitored humans taking royal jelly over a number of years. They clearly found that the research subjects benefited, some rather dramatically. They even found evidence that royal jelly delays the aging process. They achieved their results using an injectable form of royal jelly, that is they delivered the royal jelly directly into the blood. The same types of results are likely to be achieved through sublingual administration, which also leads to direct delivery. They proclaimed that those taking the royal jelly underwent "marked revitalization" of their tissues with a "visible increase" in the body's metabolism, regenerative powers, and immunity. The researchers, who were physicians, strongly believed that in the elderly royal jelly reverses joint and immune disorders. Their conclusion was that royal jelly is a "complete therapeutic" and is of "particular importance for...slowing aging." They attributed the regenerative and age-delaying actions to royal jelly's rich content of two substances: immunoglobulins and collagen precursors. The researchers stated that the immunoglobulins found in royal jelly are of "incalculable value" to health.

Yugoslavian researchers found that royal jelly is anti-viral. When combined with propolis and/or pollen, royal jelly proved effective at killing various viruses, including the herpes virus. In a study of 220 individuals the researchers determined that royal jelly and propolis exerted anti-viral actions. However, when the two were combined, the anti-viral power was accelerated substantially. Individuals given the treatment rarely suffered viral infections, while 40% of those given the placebo got sick. This large human study thoroughly proved that royal jelly is a tremendous aid to immune health.

French doctors have performed a variety of royal jelly studies. Incredibly, one study done found that women with menopausal symptoms achieved complete relief with royal jelly. What's more, there was an unexpected benefit: a few of the participants became pregnant, even though they were considered too old to conceive. This provides definitive proof that royal jelly is the most powerful regenerative substance for the endocrine system known.

In 1956 the prestigious German Medical Association did a symposium on natural cures. There, a lecture was given by H. W. Schmidt, M.D., called "Royal Jelly in Diet, Prevention, and Therapy." Dr. Schimdt proclaimed that royal jelly is indeed an effective tonic, rejuvenating the entire body. He claimed that all cells benefit from it, because it is so nutritionally rich. Royal jelly, he believed, helps normalize the functions of all organs. He attributed this effect to its rich content of hormones, enzymes, and nutrients as well as a group of substances he deemed "biocatalysts." Said Dr. Schmidt, "Royal jelly revives and stimulates the functions of cells and the secretion of glands. It accelerates the metabolism and stimulates the circulatory system. While these effects alone are rather dramatic, Dr. Schimdt continued to glorify the immense powers of this substance, saying that royal jelly "delays aging...and helps the (person) retain for as long as possible physical freshness of the body, elasticity of the mind and psychic buoyancy of youth." These are incredible statements, however, they were based on decades of German research. It is reasonable to believe the veracity of these results, because royal jelly is incredibly rich in substances desperately needed by the cells for regeneration.

According to another German physician, Hans Weitgasser, M.D., the cosmetic effects of royal jelly are dramatic. He documented numerous cases of individuals with damaged skin responding to topical application of royal jelly. Regular use, said Dr. Weitgasser, caused the "skin to become soft and wrinkles disappear." He also observed reversal of radiation damage. Dr. Weitgasser's observations, encompassing over a decade of research, illustrate the fact that royal jelly has a rather dramatic action upon the physique. He documented a case of an 18 year old female with nervousness and depression responding to royal jelly. What's more, her breast size increased dramatically. Dr. Weitgasser claimed she gained two pounds of breast tissue in three months. This could be accounted for by royal jelly's rich content of hormones. Incredibly, women with sagging breasts also responded, the tissue becoming firmer and more beautiful. Yet another woman presented with severe seborrhea of the face and scalp as well as insomnia, poor concentration, and depression. Within two months, the seborrhea was eradicated as well as the mental symptoms. What's more, this woman, who suffered from underdeveloped breasts, also developed increased mass, gaining some four centimeters (about 1 1/2 inches). The increased girth remained even after treatment was halted. Dr. Weitgasser also described the case of a 48 year old man suffering from impotence, depression, and poor concentration. Within a month after the royal jelly treatment, all symptoms were gone. Lastly, Dr. Weitgasser claimed that a number of his patients with pathological hair loss improved with royal jelly, responding with a reduction in hair loss and improved rate of growth. Greying of the hair was also reversed.

Canadian researchers published what is perhaps the most monumental study of all, even though it was only done on mice. Researchers from three of Canada's major universities found that royal jelly is one of the most potent anticancer substances known. They essentially produced a vaccine by combing the royal jelly with cancer cells. Here is how the research was performed. Investigators took mice and injected them with cancer cells: within twelve days all the mice died. Another group of mice were injected with the cancer cells plus royal jelly. These royal jelly mice all lived. All of the control mice developed tumors. All of the royal jelly mice were free of tumors. Then, months later the royal jelly mice were sacrificed, and, incredibly, they were still tumor free. Amazed by the results and conscious of the need for further proof the Canadians repeated the study numerous times on over 1,000 mice over a two year period. According to the researchers a "striking effect (was observed): Either all the mice die quickly, or all survive. Two groups of mice which received tumor cells plus royal jelly remained alive and healthy more than 12 months after inoculation, while (control) mice...died within 12 days. The results of this study were published in the prestigious magazine *Nature* in May 1959.

Case Histories

Real life human results are of critical importance in evaluating both the safety and efficacy of a substance. This is known scientifically as a "clinical trial." The results from human use, including individual uses, are highly valuable and must be considered as serious evidence of the value of a natural substance. If through taking a substance an individual experiences reversal of symptoms and/or an illness, that is monumental proof for its powers. Certain individuals might proclaim, "What about double blind studies: are they the standard?" They are the standard for evaluating drugs, which possess significant toxicity and which exhibit a well respected placebo effect. With natural substances, this procedure would be a waste of time and money. The reason is that with the vast majority of natural substances the risks for long term damage, as well as death, is minimal and in many instances nonexistent. What's more, there is a general consensus that natural substances work gradually, that is that they do not produce an immediate observable action, while drugs are expected to work quickly. Drugs affect symptoms, so this must be carefully measured to note efficacy. Natural substances aid the body in the cure. The results are obvious, that is they are easily measured and immutable, which eliminates the need for placebo. Thus, as has been determined in Germany with studies on various herbs, like St. John's wort and Gingko, the clinical study, not the double blind study, is the "gold standard" for natural substances. The fact that it works, that it eliminates symptoms, that it eradicates lesions, and/or that it reverses disease is evidence enough. Thus, the obvious powers inherent in natural substances fail to requisite double blind studies, which, while enriching universities sorely in need of research funding, offer nothing more in terms of proof than the obvious results experienced by patients.

There is another reason for the uselessness of double blind studies or other expensive research: mechanism of action. Natural substances are highly complex. They possess numerous mechanisms of action. No single mechanism can be determined. With drugs, the entire concept is to find a rather simplistic action on a specific region or organ. For instance, it is scientifically proven that royal jelly reverses aging and that it reverses fatigue. Proving "exactly" how this occurs by studying or determining the mechanism of action would cost tens of millions, perhaps billions, of dollars. Perhaps the mechanism of action will never be found. As long as it is safe and effective, that is what really matters. Royal jelly is a crude food, not a drug. Only drugs, with their high potential for fatal reactions, toxic effects, and organ damage, need to be subjected to such rigorous studies. What follows is a sprinkling of case histories, real life stories of people who have dramatically benefited from the powers of royal jelly:

Chest pain and insomnia reversed in less than an hour: Mr. C. was experiencing left-sided chest pain late at night, which kept him awake. The pain was greatly aggravated, perhaps initiated, by severe financial stress. Mr. C. was worried about a forthcoming commitment, which he feared he couldn't pay. He now worried that perhaps his heart was suffering damage. His wife observed, "You are under great stress; perhaps this is a stress reaction: take the Royal Oil." He did so by squirting about a teaspoon under the tongue. Within 10 minutes the chest pain abated, so he took another dose. Within another few minutes the pain disappeared and he fell asleep soundly. Occasionally, Mr. C. worries himself into another attack. However, as long as he takes the Royal Oil, he reduces or eliminates his stress related symptoms.

Stressed-out mother makes it home thanks to royal jelly: Mrs. D, mother of three, suffered an anxiety attack from an unknown cause. The crisis was so severe that she pulled off the road and went into a health food store. She called my office, asking for help and claiming, "I can't drive; I have my kids in the car: what do I do?" Royal jelly was prescribed. After taking it, she calmed down and was able to drive home without incident.

Lady on the verge of collapse rebounds quickly: Mrs. J. was under an enormous amount of stress due to financial pressure. She felt agitated and couldn't cope with even minimal stress. She described her dilemma as feeling "shaky" inside. Regular doses of crude royal jelly (as Royal Kick and Royal Oil) eliminated the nervousness/agitation, and she became calm within 24 hours. Plus, she experienced a dramatic increase in energy.

Salesman increases productivity 100% with royal jelly: Mr. T. is an art poster salesman who sells at trade shows. These shows are notoriously stressful and highly competitive. The energy needed to keep pace is in high demand. While his competition relied upon sugar fixes and coffee to keep pace, Mr. T. used exclusively liquid stabilized royal jelly. Incredibly, he was able to handle numerous clients simultaneously and sold an unusuallarge amount of posters, over twice his normal quota. Mr. T. always takes his royal jelly with him to trade shows, claiming it gives him a competitive edge.

Chronic fatigue syndrome improves within a week: Mrs. K was diagnosed with chronic fatigue syndrome with which she suffered for some five years. Nothing abated her symptoms. On recommendation of her physician she began taking Royal Kick, about four capsules daily in the morning. Within a week she experienced a dramatic improvement in energy. She never goes without the Royal Kick, and claims that it has cured her condition.

Woman with 30 year history of fatigue improves dramatically: Mrs. K. has suffered from fatigue and lack of muscular energy for over 30 years. She tried various nutritional supplements with only marginal results. Having nothing to lose, she decided to try Royal Kick. After only a few doses the problem was largely reversed, and she is free of the fatigue as long as she continues taking a maintenance amount. She attests that the royal jelly gives her muscular strength and allows her to work longer hours, without suffering from exhaustion. Her whole life has changed. Now, instead of collapsing in the day and sleeping, she works and accomplishes vast projects.

Jet lag prevented with liquid royal jelly: Mr. A., a prominent business executive, flies frequently. After an overseas flight, he was unable to accomplish business due to the exhaustion from severe jet lag. He no longer suffers from it, as long as he takes liquid royal jelly. He found that using the royal jelly under the tongue repeatedly was the best technique for obliterating jet lag.

Ten years of disability eliminated: Ms. P., a 23 year old university student, suffered from one of the most debilitating of all conditions: severe endometriosis. She had tried every known therapy to no avail. She was taking the appropriate drugs, but saw no hope in a cure. I told her about royal jelly, so she began taking fortified royal jelly religiously, about six capsules daily. Within a week she noticed a significant reduction in the pain. Within two months, the condition was eradicated. Note: Ms. P. also took high quality northern Pacific kelp to boost her thyroid function, along with oil of oregano as an antifungal.

Blood sugar swings halted rapidly: Ms. D. is a chocolate addict who suffers severe blood sugar fluctuations. The blood sugar swings were so debilitating that she was often bedridden. She tried a variety of herbs and B vitamin supplements with minimal if any results. Within a week of taking the Royal Kick she noticed a significant difference: less dizziness and a reduction in lightheaded sensations. Plus, the Royal Kick gives her great physical strength, and she is able to accomplish tasks that previously were impossible. Now she relies on the Royal Kick to keep her blood sugar in balance and is able to lead a normal life.

"Kidney" pain eliminated within an hour: Mr. K. suffered bouts of pain in the mid-lower back which he described as "over the kidneys." The pain worsened when he was under stress. It was a sharp pain, but it didn't feel like a sore muscle or joint. He learned that it was probably adrenal pain, so to counteract it he took the royal jelly. Incredibly, within an hour the pain was significantly diminished. Whenever the pain returns he relies on the powers of royal jelly, finding that this therapy consistently eliminates it.

Debilitating hip pain helped by fortified royal jelly: Mrs. K., a 52 year old woman, has chronic hip pain caused by a serious fall. The pain is so extreme on occasion that it takes her breath away. She tried calcium pills and other supplements but to no avail. Crude, fortified royal jelly was administered; after only one dose she noticed an improvement in her stamina and strength. Within an hour the pain improved. While the hip pain is far from cured, she reports that as long as she takes royal jelly, the pain is bearable, diminished by as much as 50%. Plus, she can move more freely, a benefit she attributes directly to the royal jelly.

Menopausal symptoms abated: Ms. D. is a 49 year old female suffering from the typical symptoms of menopausal syndrome— hot flashes, sweaty, fatigue, irratability and more. Then she began regularly using Royal Oil, taking 1 teaspoon in hot water daily. Within ten days she noticed that the menopausal symptoms were abated. She is pleased with how she feels and continues to take Royal Oil.

Conclusion

The medicinal powers of royal jelly have only recently been revealed. This substance is of immense value, although relatively few individuals are taking advantage of it. Perhaps this is because it is not a drug, that is it operates through a completely different mechanism. Rather than altering a specific function or modifying a specific symptom, it acts through a holistic mechanism. In fact, it acts upon the entire body, a mechanism with which modern medicine is unfamiliar. Its purpose is not to suddenly or magically reverse a symptom, although it may do so. Rather, it serves to gradually replenish vital substances which nourish the cells: hormones, enzymes, vitamins, minerals, amino acids, and other potent factors. Through these critical and difficult to procure substances it revitalizes the cells and organs of the body.

While royal jelly offers curative properties, it is not a drug. It isn't even an herb. It is a food-like substance. Thus, it operates by nourishing body. Royal jelly fails to cure disease. However, it boosts the reserves and potencies of the human cells and organs. In other words, it helps the body cure itself. Thus, royal jelly is merely the fuel that gives the body the opportunity to heal, to eradicate toxicity, infection, and disease itself. The body possesses remarkable healing properties. Royal jelly is the body's assistant, aiding it in its miraculous curative work. This explains why royal jelly is useful in virtually any illness.

Royal jelly increases the body's resistance to disease. This alone makes it a worthy tonic. Once it is established, disease is difficult to eradicate. The ideal approach is to prevent it from striking, and this is where royal jelly is crucial. By nourishing, rebuilding, and reviving the cells, it builds the body's resistance. In other words, it helps the body create healthy tissue. Plus, it assists the body in repairing damaged tissue. In contrast, drugs usually disrupt the cells, damaging and even destroying them, which thus leads to ill health.

Royal jelly is the only food supplement proven to stimulate tired or weakened organs, revive their functions and rejuvenate their cells. It does so gently. Rarely does anyone notice a sudden or "wired" effect. It is also the only natural substance proven to retard the aging process, a benefit that is observable both in blood chemistry and in the obvious appearance, behavior, and vitality of the individual.

The nutritional profile of royal jelly is immense. A search of the scientific literature proves that no other known substance matches it. It contains vitamins, minerals, coenzymes, catalysts, amino acids, collagen precursors, immunogloblulins, albumin, minerals, phospholipids, essential fatty acids, steroids, nucleic acids, and neurotransmitters. Many of these substances are found in no other food or medicine. In short, it contains everything the body needs to thrive.

Think about this from the cells' point of view. The cells must have a complete repertoire of nutrients to survive: to resist breakdown and to revive. If even a single substance is lacking, the cells are weakened. If the deficiency is prolonged, cells may become diseased, perhaps die. When royal jelly is consumed, the cell can draw on the nutrients it provides, absorbing critical factors, like DNA and RNA, or some direly needed substance. For the cell this infusion could mean the difference between life and death. For ideal benefit the infusion must be delivered regularly, that is daily.

In the past taste intolerance prevented individuals from complying with royal jelly therapy. What's more, using fresh royal jelly is cumbersome, because it must be refrigerated, since it spoils easily. Those issues have now been resolved. Crude stabilized royal jelly is available. Unopened, it has a shelf life of nearly a year and when refrigerated after opening may last even longer. However, the purpose is to consume it. With proper consumption about two ounces should last no more than a month.

Stabilized royal jelly delivers additional benefits versus the commercial fresh type, because it contains natural antioxidants. These antioxidants, made from spices, help deliver the active ingredients of the royal jelly directly into the blood. Thus, the individual receives the greatest impact possible from this rare and valuable substance.

Royal jelly is one of the most well tolerated of all supplements. It is also one of the purest. With high grade products there is little or no chance for adulteration. Plus, with genetically engineered foods corrupting the food supply it is reassuring to know that in the case of royal jelly the bees are the engineers. In other words, it is free of man-made corruption.

High grade royal jelly products are usually more expensive than the commercial varieties. It simply costs more to procure high quality raw materials. There are dozens of grades of royal jelly. The Royal Kick and Royal Oil contain only the highest grade royal jelly available: guaranteed.

Do not use inferior grades of royal jelly or capsules containing potentially allergenic ingredients, like wheat germ or soy. Some companies even put antifreeze and food dyes in their capsules.

Use only products free of additives and which guarantee high original levels of the active ingredient: 10-HDA. The level must originate at a minimum of 5.0% and, preferably, at least 6.0% or the product is inferior grade.

Often, the expectations with a natural compound are high. A fast result is expected. The fact is the individual should expect results within a reasonable period. However, when using royal jelly, be patient. Remember, the goal is to assist the body in regeneration. The body may be severely deficient, and it may take time to induce regeneration. In an individual who is severely depleted it may take a month or two for regeneration to begin. Follow your symptoms using the deficiency tests. Ask friends if they notice a change. Here is a helpful rule: for every year an individual is ill, it may take a month to notice differences. For instance, for a person who is ill for 12 years it may take ten months to a year for obvious improvement to be noticed. This means that the body is gradually healing, but it needs a significant amount of time on the therapy to completely recover. With royal jelly therapy significant results should be seen within 90 days.

Chapter 5

Preventive Medicine

Prevention is an important concept. Today, virtually anyone could develop a sudden illness and/or infection. This makes the 21st century a frightening time in modern history. In the Western world the cancer incidence is frighteningly high. During the 21st century it is predicted that as many as one in two individuals will be stricken with some form of cancer during his/her lifetime. Once cancer strikes, it is difficult to reverse. This is also true of other degenerative diseases, like Alzheimer's disease, Parkinsonism, diabetes, arthritis, and heart disease. The ideal approach is to prevent such disease from happening. This is where royal jelly is so versatile. Regardless of the disease, it helps strengthen the resistance which aids the body in its attempts to recover. Ideally, it should be taken regularly to resist disease before it strikes. Royal jelly helps make the cells as healthy as possible. This is because it is the most potent food supplement known. While it is not a cancer cure, the regular intake will help keep the body in top nutritional condition. As a result, the vulnerability to the development of serious illnesses, including cancer, arthritis, Alzheimer's disease, diabetes, and heart disease, will diminish.

Athletic Stamina

Royal jelly is highly versatile for enhancing athletic performance. Athletes should expect to notice a major impact, virtually immediately. The increased power and stamina can be dramatic. Certainly, mental acuity and focus will improve, but so will physical strength and stamina. For particularly tough events take the royal jelly several times daily, like every two or three hours in order to maintain significant blood levels. Also, take it right before the event. Depending on the activity, such as competitions or marathons, you may take it during the event.

Pregnancy

Many women are afraid of taking supplements or herbs during this critical time. There is some justification to this. Yet, pregnant women often eat atrocious food without thought. there are countless junk food babies. True, a few herbs must be avoided during pregnancy, however, many are safe, in fact, health enhancing. Royal jelly is a food, so it is completely safe. In fact, it dramatically enhances the health of the developing baby as well as the mother. Royal jelly contains certain vitamins which are difficult to procure from regular food, like pantothenic acid and pyridoxine. Plus, it provides natural hormones which nourish the glands, and this is vital for the creation of a healthy baby. Royal jelly is a rich source of phospholipids, direly needed for the developing nervous system as well as lungs. Take royal jelly without concern: the health of the developing baby and the mother's body may depend upon it.

In order to have the healthiest baby possible, take high quality royal jelly products, like Royal Oil and Royal Kick, as much as is needed to improve physical strength and stamina. Royal jelly may also be helpful for that disconcerting complaint: nausea of pregnancy. Simply take 2 or more capsules of Royal Kick with every meal: results should be immediate.

Raw honey is also safe to consume during pregnancy. It is an effective aid to an upset stomach as well as constipation and diarrhea. Honey boosts immune strength, both for the mother and developing baby. It is the safe sweet food for pregnancy. In contrast, refined sugar is damaging. Crude raw honey nourishes the body. Refined sugar depletes nutrients. Natural honey balances the nerves. Refined sugar weakens the nerves, causing fatigue, irritability, anxiety, depression, mood swings, yeast infections, and numerous other symptoms.

Breast feeding

Royal jelly is perhaps the most potent breast milk supplement known. It boosts milk flow while increasing its nutritional value. Royal jelly is a complete food. It fills nutritional gaps resulting from improper diet. It provides small but important doses of all of the B vitamins. What's more, it provides a variety of biological substances which aid immune function. When the nursing mother consumes royal jelly, these immune factors are transferred to the baby. For ideal absorption take the royal jelly under the tongue.

Royal jelly can dramatically improve the health and beauty of the infant. It helps enrich the infant's skin and thicken his/her hair, plus it bolsters the baby's immunity. Use stabilized royal jelly on a daily basis. The long term results could be glorious.

Immune Health

The strength of the immune system may falter for a variety of reasons. For instance, as we age the function of the immune system declines. The elderly are particularly vulnerable to serious infections. A relatively healthy individual may suddenly become ill and possibly die because of a vulnerable or aged immune system. In the elderly, germs attack easily, because the immune system lacks the tools to respond to the assault.

Nutritional deficiencies also weaken immunity. A lack of vitamins, minerals, amino acids, and essential fatty acids increases the risks for infections.

Immunity may also be disabled by drugs. The regular intake of potent medications depresses the immune system. Drugs which are particularly toxic to the immune system include aspirin, ibuprofen, antibiotics, heart drugs, cholesterol-lowering drugs, arthritis medications, and cortisone.

Royal jelly provides the missing factors needed to keep the immune system healthy. Its rich content of pantothenic acid and amino acids greatly bolsters white blood cell, as well as immunoglobulin, synthesis. It provides natural antibiotics as well as immunoglobulins. Royal jelly is the richest natural source of gamma globulin. Drs. Lamberti and Cornello of Argentina claim this royal jelly globulin is of "incalculable importance" to human health. Consume royal jelly to keep your immune system in top shape. Take at least 2 capsules of the stabilized/fortified powder along with a few drops of the liquid every day.

Raw honey is also an ideal tonic for immune health. Bee keepers are the longest lived profession. I personally know numerous beekeepers who are over 90, and they are vigorous. As a preventive medicine take a teaspoon or two of crude raw honey daily. Wild honey offers the greatest medicinal powers. Crude wild honey strengthens the immune system, reducing the risks for infections as well as allergic reactions. For more information or to order high quality raw honeys see the Web site, MedicinalHoneys.com, or call 1-800-243-5242.

Of course, there is always a chance that a person might be allergic to something. If you are not sure about how well you can tolerate bee products, start using them in tiny amounts, gradually increasing the amounts to tolerance. Or, begin using them by placing a tiny amount under the tongue. If there is no reaction, gradually increase the amount until you take safely take them with in any quantity. There are those who may tolerate one bee product and not another. Allergy or intolerance is rare, but always be aware that every person is different and each person's physiology has its own idiosyncrasies. Rarely, allergic intolerance to royal jelly may occur. It is more common with bee pollen. In either case if you start with tiny amounts by putting it under the tongue tolerance may be created. Or, take a tiny amount of raw honey under the tongue, and gradually increase this until your tolerance for other bee products improves. If you do have a history of severe reactions, know that there are antidotes. The Oreganol or Oregacyn are the finest. For any reaction, mild or severe, simply take a few drops of Oreganol under the tongue or a few capsules of the Oregacyn. The allergic/toxic reaction will be rapidly halted.

Our immune systems are under great duress, to a greater degree than any time previously. Bizarre diseases are striking millions of individuals. No one is immune. Health is a valuable commodity. Keep it in top order through the powers of royal jelly and wild honey.

Hormonal health

Hormones are highly specialized substances which exert potent effects upon the cells and organs. The hormones control a huge number of cellular functions. The hormones are vital. Without them, the body becomes diseased and death may result.

Hormones are produced by a number of glands, which are collectively called the endocrine glands. These glands include the thyroid, adrenals, ovaries, testes, pituitary, and pineal. All of these glands produce their own repertoire of hormones.

Aging has been proven to be caused largely by a decline in hormone levels. For instance, a low level of the adrenal hormone DHEA is a marker of accelerated aging. Levels of sex hormones also decline with aging. When hormone levels are increased, signs of aging are diminished, perhaps reversed. Royal jelly is a type of natural hormone replacement therapy. In contrast to drugs it provides hormonal support for the entire endocrine system. This means that royal jelly boosts the function of all of the hormonal glands. It is particularly effective at enhancing the production of adrenal hormones, although it is also a potent sex hormone inducer. Healthy glands mean a healthy, vital body. This ability to revitalize the glands makes royal jelly unique in comparison to all other nutritional supplements.

Pets

Royal jelly is one of the safest medicines for pets. It can be given in the powdered or liquid form. Pets benefit greatly, as is illustrated by improved appearance and vigor. Irene Stein, in her book, *Royal Jelly: The New Guide to Nature's Richest Health Food*, reports that pets generally respond to royal jelly with an increase in vigor, vitality, and energy, plus if they have nervous disorders, they become more calm. She relates dozens of conditions which have responded to royal jelly therapy, including unhealthy coat, poor appetite, emphysema, sluggish kidneys, hair loss, bladder infections, constipation, joint disorders, and allergies. The Royal Oil is easiest to take. Simply mix a small amount, like a half teaspoon, in wet food or water. Or, open a capsule of the dried powder and add to wet food. Use as much as is necessary to achieve the desired effect.

Mental energy

Having sufficient mental energy is defined as the power to use the mind to its maximum capacity. The brain uses a greater amount of energy than any other organ. Symptoms of a lack of mental energy include poor concentration, memory loss, confusion, anxiety, depression, agitation, and irritability.

The elderly commonly experience a decline in mental powers. However, what is rather astonishing is that this is occurring in young adults, even children. The primary cause is nutritional deficiency, as well as a deficiency in key substances which activate the brain, that is the neurotransmitters. Royal jelly is rich in the nutrients needed by the brain, plus it contains a number of neurotransmitters. These chemicals are quickly absorbed by the brain, activating its functions. Thus, it is expected that the regular intake of royal jelly will rejuvenate mental capacity, leading to clarity in thinking, improved concentration, and enhanced memory.

Children and teenagers also suffer from poor mental performance. This is often reflected in problems at school or poor grades. In many instances the diets of these youngsters are devoid of the critical nutrients required by the brain for normal function. For instance, refined sugar destroys nutrients. It rapidly depletes critical minerals like magnesium and calcium. It also depletes thiamine, niacin, pyridoxine, and pantothenic acid, all of which are direly needed by brain cells. The brain continues to develop even through the late teens. It requires intensive nourishment to function at an optimal level. Royal jelly provides many of the nutrients needed by the developing brain. It also provides nutrition for the function of the physique, including the hormone system. The so called lazy child who is a poor performer in school may dramatically benefit from royal jelly. For children or teenagers with behavioral disorders the results of royal jelly therapy may be dramatic: improved mood, better attitude, increased stamina, less truancy, and higher test scores.

Daily energy

This is something everyone needs. There is so much to do in modern life, but is there enough energy? Many people claim they feel great. However, when you examine their history and symptoms, energy is lacking. The lack of energy is often disguised by a sort of boldness or, perhaps, denial. Or, it may be masked by certain habits which create false energy, like cigarette smoking, coffee drinking, chocolate consumption, or even recreational drug use. People use stimulants to gain a false sensation of energy. If the individual failed to use stimulants, he/she would probably collapse.

What is lacking is energy reserve. The cells and organs are exhausted, and they must constantly be provoked in order for the individual to have enough energy to make it through the day. Determining the "energy reserve" is a simple way to discover what is your energy status. A test has been devised to determine what is your energy reserve.

Take the following test. Answer each question carefully, trying to be as objective and accurate as possible. Often, it helps to take this test with a friend, which may aid objectivity. Add the points to determine your score.

Which of these applies to you:

- set alarm but usually don't get up (2)
- wake up from alarm (or other provocation) but usually go

back to sleep (2)
- get tired after eating or feel sleepy after eating (1)
- chocolate consumption
  - ---not very often 0
  - ---often, like a few times per month 1
  - ---frequently, like a few times per week 2
  - ---fairly large amounts, like every day 3
  - ---large amounts; several times per day 5
- feel jittery inside (1)
- poor memory (1)
- don't have the energy for love making (1)
- muscles tire easily from minor exercise (2)
- take sleeping pills on a daily or weekly basis...2
- need exercise to increase energy...2
- constantly yawning...1
- always behind at work...1
- tons of energy at night but no energy in the morning...1
- fall asleep sitting up...1
- get a buzz from caffeine...1
- sugar makes you depressed...2
- get wired from sugar...2
- fall asleep at work...2
- suffer from narcolepsy ...2
- get tired when driving...1
- constantly crave sugar...1
- constantly crave alcohol...2
- alcohol consumption
  - ---rarely or none 0
  - ---occasionally, like a few per month...1
  - ---often, like a few per week.....2
  - ---a few drinks per day.....3
  - ---six or more drinks per day...4
- use "recreational drugs" for a high...

    ---daily...6
    ---weekly..4
    ---occasionally..2
- cigarette smoking
    ---occasionally..1
    ---a few packs per week,,3
    ---a pack per day...4
    ---over a pack or up to two packs per day...5
    ---three or more packs per day...7
- fall asleep watching TV...1
- can't relax (1)
- get tired when reading (1)
- constantly complain about being tired (2)
- worry incessantly (1)
- take prescription drugs daily (2)
- procrastinate about doing chores...1
- hate the though of exercising...1
- never exercise...2
- muscle fatigue...2
- hard time walking up steps..1
- get short of breath easily...2
- leg cramps...1
- hate the thought of going to work or school..1
- always behind on school work....1
- feel lazy constantly...1
- avoid doing heavy work due to fatigue...1
- make excuses for not helping do chores when asked...1
- must have a coffee, pop, or cola in the morning..3
- eat sugar for a rise...3
- eat chocolate for energy...2
- feel tired after eating...1
- coffee consumption:
    ---only occasionally 0

---about a cup per day   1
---two or three cups daily   3
---four or five cups daily   4
---six to nine cups daily   5
---10 or more cups daily   6]
- have a need to avoid stress of any kind
- sensitive to sound
- easily irritated
- inability to concentrate
- fail to finish jobs and/or assignments
- get involved in road rage often
- feel violently or uncontrollably angry
- body is tense and constricted constantly

0 to 5 points: Excellent reserve

Your cellular energy reserves are intact. As a result, you can handle an extensive amount of work without suffering from fatigue. In other words, you have a high degree of stamina.

6 to 9 points: Good reserve

Your cellular energy is acceptable, but it can improve. You can handle a fair amount of stress and are accomplishing demanding work without serious fatigue. However, prolonged stress or an excessive work load could lead to exhaustion. People with this score may occasionally rely on caffeine or other stimulants for a boost. Royal jelly naturally boosts energy, so if this is taken regularly, there is no need for stimulants. It provides nuclear material, that is naturally occurring DNA and RNA, so your body's internal "nuclear generators" can be revived.

10 to 15: Poor reserve

You are suffering from a depletion of cellular energy. It is likely that you are suffering from deficiencies of energizing nutrients, like the B complex as well as magnesium. Stress and intense work projects further deplete your reserves. The cells can be replenished by improving the diet, eliminating stimulants, and taking royal jelly. Alcohol, sugar, caffeine, and chocolate must be strictly avoided. Royal jelly naturally boosts energy, so if this is taken regularly, there is no need for stimulants. It provides nuclear material, that is naturally occurring DNA and RNA, so your body's internal "nuclear generators" can be revived. It also provides neurotransmitters, which help activate a sluggish brain. Royal jelly is one of the few nutritional supplements that can safely boost the body's ability to produce energy.

16 to 23 Minimal reserve

You are suffering from a cellular energy drain. Perhaps the energy you do have is coming from raw will power and/or stimulants. The stimulants are counterproductive, because they further deplete the needed cellular energizers. Deficiencies of B vitamins and trace minerals, particularly magnesium and phosphorus, are probably rampant. Thiamine deficiency is of particular concern. This B vitamin is required for the creation of cellular energy. Alcohol, sugar, caffeine, and chocolate must be strictly avoided. These toxins deplete from the body the nutrients it needs for energy. Royal jelly naturally boosts energy, so if it is taken regularly, there is no need for stimulants. It provides nuclear material, that is DNA and RNA, so your body's internal "nuclear generators" can be revived. The intake of royal jelly on a daily basis revitalizes the cells and brings energy reservoirs to optimal levels. It also provides neurotransmitters, which help activate a sluggish brain.

24 to 31: Virtually no reserve

You are suffering from severe cellular exhaustion. This increases the risks of a variety of diseases, including heart disease, chronic fatigue syndrome, fibromyalgia, depression, anxiety, panic attacks, and immune deficiency. There are probably dozens of physical and mental drains against your reserves, including demanding work, worry, poor diet, and stress. Halt all stimulants immediately. Curtail the intake of alcohol. Warning: a sudden withdrawal of the stimulants may lead to collapse; your body is dependent upon these poisons for energy. So, eliminate them gradually if you are at risk of collapsing. Also, prescription drugs deplete cellular energy. See your doctor about reducing/eliminating intake. Stimulants, as well as drugs, destroy nutrients. For instance, coffee depletes magnesium, aspirin destroys vitamin C, and diuretics induce the loss of potassium, sodium, and magnesium. All of these nutrients are required by the body for energy synthesis.

Natural remedies are reliable aids for bolstering energy reserves. Take a B complex tablet along with magnesium. Thiamine deficiency is of particular concern. This B vitamin is required for the creation of cellular energy. Natural sources of thiamine include royal jelly, crude rice polish, rice germ, liver, and yeast extract. Eat healthy salty snacks, like pickles, olives, salted roasted nuts, and salted chicken parts (not fried nugget type). The salt boosts adrenal function, helping to reverse fatigue. Consume royal jelly every day until the energy reserves are rebuilt. Take large amounts, like several capsules and/or teaspoons daily. For further information regarding your nutritional status see the Web site, NutritionTest.com.

32 and above: Complete lack of reserve

Danger zone: the degree of cellular exhaustion is monumental. The cells of your body are desperately in need of support. The body is vulnerable to a breakdown in the hormone system as well as immune system. There is an increased risk for the development of diabetes, heart disease, chronic fatigue syndrome, depression, anxiety, panic attacks, and fibromyalgia.

For energy don't rely upon toxic stimulants, like caffeine, sugar, iced tea, black tea, and chocolate. The result of consuming these foods/beverages is a further depletion of energy. The use of stimulants must be halted so that the cellular energy reserves can be rebuilt. Strictly avoid alcohol consumption. Prescription drugs interfere with the cells' ability to synthesize energy. See your doctor about reducing intake. Note: stimulants and drugs destroy nutrients, particularly B vitamins and trace minerals. If you have a history of persistent use of prescription drugs, alcohol, and/or stimulants, take B complex along with extra potassium and magnesium. B vitamins are required for the creation of cellular energy. Thiamine is particularly important for boosting cellular energy. Natural sources of thiamine include royal jelly, crude rice polish, rice germ, liver, and yeast extract. Nutri-Sense powder is a special type of natural thiamine source, plus it is rich in natural niacin. This nutritious powder is made from crude rice fractions and crushed organic flax seed. To correct thiamine and/or niacin deficiency take three heaping tablespoons once or twice daily. It may be added to yogurt or cereal. Or, add it to soup just before serving. The Nutri-Sense plus royal jelly capsules provides the natural B vitamins your body so desperately needs.

To correct the energy depletion the diet must be dramatically altered. Strictly avoid the consumption of processed foods, and eat fresh organic meat, poultry, fish, vegetables, milk products, eggs, and fruit. Eat healthy salty snacks, like pickles, olives, salted roasted nuts, and salted chicken parts. The salt boosts adrenal function, helping to reverse fatigue. Be aware that sudden withdrawal of coffee may provoke headaches. However, take the royal jelly to aid in any withdrawals. Royal jelly provides the nutrients craved by the cells for their survival, including all of the B vitamins. Pantothenic acid, of which it is rich, is known as the "energy vitamin." It supplies nuclear material, that is naturally occurring DNA and RNA, so your body's internal "nuclear generators" can be revived. Take royal jelly every day in order to revitalize your cells and bring energy reservoirs to their optimal levels.

Nutritional deficiency is an epidemic, afflicting virtually all North Americans. The American diet, with its emphasis on processed, fast, synthetic, genetically engineered, and packaged foods, is notoriously defective nutritionally. Mental and physical fatigue are common consequences of this insufficient nutrition. What's more, fad and trendy diets also create nutritional deficiencies. A diet heavily emphasizing soy, grains, fruit, or raw vegetables leads to nutritional deficiencies. Virtually all vegetarians suffer significant vitamin/mineral deficiencies, even if they supplement the diet. Regarding fatigue, the major nutrients lacking include potassium, magnesium, copper, iron, cobalt, vitamin B-12, pantothenic acid, thiamine, niacin, and pyridoxine. If you suffer from a history of chronic fatigue, that is physical and/or mental exhaustion, take the highly detailed NutritionTests to see where you stand. It is always a better idea to know what the nutritional deficiencies are before supplementing.

Now you know where you stand from an intracellular point of view. Use the test to measure your response to royal jelly. While consuming the Royal Kick and/or Royal Oil, take the energy reserve test repeatedly, like once per month, that is until you score in the excellent range. That will be the evidence that the royal jelly has revived and regenerated your cells.

Conclusion

The powers of royal jelly are immense. It is one of those rare natural substances which can help people get well rapidly. It is powerful yet subtle, strong yet gentle, and valuable yet cost effective.

Royal jelly has the power to change lives, mentally and physically. This is because it improves overall health, in other words, it helps the individual function better. It also improves appearance, making the skin prettier and healthier. Not all royal jelly is the same. Quality matters immensely. Plus, the royal jelly must be preserved properly, otherwise it degenerates. Use only 100% pure, unprocessed royal jelly without harmful additives. Avoid inferior quality royal jelly products or those containing disruptive additives, like wheat, corn, or soy by-products, preservatives, or emulsifiers. Thus, the royal jelly must be in a pure state, or, it must be fortified with natural substances which enhance its power. Be sure that the manufacturer certifies that the royal jelly it uses is free of all chemical additives and adulterants.

The process of fortification increases the potency and utility of royal jelly. It may be fortified with pantothenic acid as well as fatty acids. The addition of crude natural vitamin C in the form of acerola cherry extract is also a means of fortification, since royal jelly is lacking in this nutrient. Fortification creates a superior product, giving royal jelly that additional edge for improving health.

When compared to other herbal or nutritional tonics, royal jelly has decided advantages. For instance, commercial herbal medicines tend to be specific in their actions. Rather than working on a specific condition or region of the body, royal jelly, boosts the function of all cells. It regenerates tissues and organs, and this function is difficult to gain in the typical herbal formulas. Plus, it provides a dense amount of nutrients, many of which are difficult to procure elsewhere. What's more, it is one of the few natural hormonal tonics available.

Currently, tens of thousands of individuals are raving about the benefits they are receiving from royal jelly therapy. It is most famous in Europe as a remedy for physical strength and energy as well as enhanced beauty. In this fast pace life the individual needs a tonic, such as royal jelly, to keep pace with stress and/or imbalanced nutrition. There is no means for the average individual to procure the variety of nutrients he/she needs. If the diet is deficient, royal jelly fills some of the gaps.

The benefits of the regular intake of royal jelly are immense. These benefits include improved energy, greater physical strength, increased tolerance to stress, better mood, healthier skin, and improved concentration. Royal jelly added to the daily diet is likely to have an enormous impact on well-being, physically and mentally. Royal jelly increases the natural strength of the cells, greatly improving their resistance to disease. As a result, the health improvements may be immense. Thus, the body can function at the most optimal level possible. Take advantage of this potent and highly nourishing substance. Your life may depend upon it.

Conclusion

The powers of royal jelly are immense. It is one of those rare natural substances which can help people get well rapidly. It is powerful yet subtle, strong yet gentle, and valuable yet cost effective.

Royal jelly has the power to change lives, mentally and physically. This is because it improves overall health, in other words, it helps the individual function better. It also improves appearance, making the skin prettier and healthier. Not all royal jelly is the same. Quality matters immensely. Plus, the royal jelly must be preserved properly, otherwise it degenerates. Use only 100% pure, unprocessed royal jelly without harmful additives. Avoid inferior quality royal jelly products or those containing disruptive additives, like wheat, corn, or soy by-products, preservatives, or emulsifiers. Thus, the royal jelly must be in a pure state, or, it must be fortified with natural substances which enhance its power. Be sure that the manufacturer certifies that the royal jelly it uses is free of all chemical additives and adulterants.

The process of fortification increases the potency and utility of royal jelly. It may be fortified with pantothenic acid as well as fatty acids. The addition of crude natural vitamin C in the form of acerola cherry extract is also a means of fortification, since royal jelly is lacking in this nutrient. Fortification creates a superior product, giving royal jelly that additional edge for improving health.

When compared to other herbal or nutritional tonics, royal jelly has decided advantages. For instance, commercial herbal medicines tend to be specific in their actions. Rather than working on a specific condition or region of the body, royal jelly boosts the function of all cells. It regenerates tissues and organs, and this function is difficult to gain in the typical herbal formulas. Plus, it provides a dense amount of nutrients, many of which are difficult to procure elsewhere. What's more, it is one of the few natural hormonal tonics available.

Currently, tens of thousands of individuals are raving about the benefits they are receiving from royal jelly therapy. It is most famous in Europe as a remedy for physical strength and energy as well as enhanced beauty. In this fast pace life the individual needs a tonic, such as royal jelly, to keep pace with stress and/or imbalanced nutrition. There is no means for the average individual to procure the variety of nutrients he/she needs. If the diet is deficient, royal jelly fills some of the gaps.

The benefits of the regular intake of royal jelly are immense. These benefits include improved energy, greater physical strength, increased tolerance to stress, better mood, healthier skin, and improved concentration. Royal jelly added to the daily diet is likely to have an enormous impact on well-being, physically and mentally. Royal jelly increases the natural strength of the cells, greatly improving their resistance to disease. As a result, the health improvements may be immense. Thus, the body can function at the most optimal level possible. Take advantage of this potent and highly nourishing substance. Your life may depend upon it.

Real Life Stories—The Evidence

February 25, 2001

Dr. Cass Ingram
North American Herb & Spice
P.O. Box 4885
Buffalo Grove, IL 60089

Dear Dr. Ingram:

I enjoyed your lecture at the Victoria Health Show. I found it interesting and informative. Most of all it confirmed my thoughts of what is happening in the health field today.

I have been a believer of alternative medicine for twenty five years and truly believe that grandma knew best. I look forward to the day when food will once more become medicine and doctors will practice preventing disease. I applaud you for your good work.

I would like to share my Royal Kick experience with you.

I had been fighting the flu bug for several weeks and then did succumb to it for a couple of days. This left me tired, listless and irritable. I would sleep for twelve hours yet felt as if I had not slept at all. After your lecture at the Health Show I purchased some Royal Kick and the next morning began taking six capsules with my breakfast. After two days I could feel a change in my body. My energy level was increasing and I felt better than I had in months. By the end of the week I felt as if my whole body had been transformed. It was as though all the cells in my body were jumping for joy. I felt so alive. That feeling of "well being" was and still is wonderful. This is how one is supposed to feel. An added bonus is that I do not have as much anxiety as I did prior to taking Royal Kick. Royal Kick is truly an incredible food supplement. I have taken other Royal Jelly but none of them has done for me what Royal Kick has. It will always be a part of my daily routine. V.L.P.

I am looking forward to your book on Royal Jelly. I will look for it at The Vitamin Shop.

Sincerely,

Dear Doctor Cass,

*I would like to thank you for introducing the wonderful Royal oil and\\
Royal kick products into my life. I will forever spread the good word.*

*A wonderful friend mentioned that due to my sluggish thyroid
condition it would be recommended that I take 10 to 12 capsules a day
plus 2 teaspoons or more of royal oil. I also found the self- test nutrition
guide book was extremely helpful in finding out my nutritional
deficiency's and treating them accordingly. I was also told that after
awhile I will not feel tired and weak in the morning and would naturally
wake up early with energy.*

*Well I have been following this program consistently for two months
now and I have arrived to that unexplainable point. I have been
transformed! I feel alert full of energy and have a clarity that I have never
felt before. A heavy cloud has been lifted away. I also feel as though I
have halted my aging process to a certain point. I am so excited because I
know that royal jelly has so many other lovely properties that I will find
out through educating myself.*

GOD BLESS THE BEES!!

Thank you,

Courtney Contos

Bibliography

Abd-Alla, M. S., Mishref, A., and I. M. Ghazi. 1995. Antimicrobial potency of royal jelly collected from queen cells at different larvae ages. *Annals of Agric. Science* (Cairo). 2:597-608.

Aagaard, K. L. 1974. *The Natural Product Propolis—the Way to Health.* Denmark: Mentor Publ.

Barton-Wright, E. C. and W. A. Elliot. 1963. The pantothenic acid metabolism of rheumatoid arthritis. *The Lancet:* Oct 26th.

Bergman, A., et al. 1983. Acceleration of wound healing by topical application of honey. *Amer. J. Surg.* V: 145 (March).

Broadhurst, C. L. 1999. Bee Products: Medicine from the Hive. *Nutrition Science News.* August, pp. 366-67.

Brown, R. 1993. *Royden Brown's Bee Hive Product Bible.* New York: Avery Publ.

Ferlat, S., et al. 1994. Immunomodulating properties of hydroxy-20 decen 2 transoic aid and glycerol derivatives on a macrophage cell line. *Travaux Scientifiques des Chercheurs du Service de Sante des Armees.* 15:161-162.

Hayes, L. J. and R. A. Baldensnerger. 1958. Bees sterilize pollen by means of a glandular secretion which is antagonistic to tumors. *L'Apiculteur halt-chinois.*

Hill, R. 1977. *Propolis: the Natural Antibiotic.* London: Thoorsons.

Inoue, T. 1982. Royal jelly as a folk medicine. *Mitsubachi Kagaku (Honeybee Science).* 3:15-18.

Ivanov, T. and B. Mitev. 1980. Composition and physiocochemical properties of royal jelly. *Zhivotnov dni Nauki.* 17: 89-95.

Kaftanoglu, O. and A. Tanyeli. 1997. The use of royal jelly during treatment of childhood malignancies. Conference Proc. New York: Penum Publ.

Kitzes, G. and H. A. Scheulte. J. Nutr. 26(241).

Kramer, K.J., et al. 1982. Purification of insulin-like peptides from insect haemolymph and royal jelly. *Insect Biochemistry.*

Lecker, G., et al. 1982. Components of royal jelly II: the lipid fraction, hydrocarbons and sterols. *J. Apic. Res.* 21:1, 178.

Lyngheim, L. and J. Scagnetti. 1979. *Bee Pollen: Nature's Miracle Health Food.* Whilshire Book Co.

Makarov, F. D. *Propolis Therapy:The Healing Art.* USSR:#4.

Mizrahi, A. and Y. Lensky. 1997. Bee products, properties, applications, and apitherapy. In: abstracts and proceedings, New York: Plenum Press.

Nassis, C., et al. 1998. In vivo study of antimycotic activity of royal jelly. *Anais Brasileiros de Dermatologia.* 73:167.

Novellio, J. D. and F. Lipman. 1947. *J. Biol. Chem.*

Paoos, E. and C. Andrei. 1978. Royal jelly, a fortifying apitherapeutic product. *Apicultura in Romania.* 55(11).

Popeskowic, D., et al. 1998. The contemporar aspects of finalization and utilization of honeybee products. *Veterinarskin Glasnik.* 52:331-336.

Shils, M. E. 1951. *Archives Biochem.* 32(227).

Soliman, F. A. and A. Soliman. 1957. The gonad stimulating potency of date palm pollen grains. *Experentia* (October).

Stein, Irene. 1989. *Royal Jelly: The New Guide to Nature's Richest Health Food.* Wellngborough: Thorson's

Vittek, J. and B. L. Slomiany. 1984. Testosterone in royal jelly. *Experientia.* Vol. 40.

Vittek, J. 1995. Effect of royal jelly on serum lipids in experimental animals and humans with atheroscerosis. *Experientia.* 51:927.

Wade, Carlson. 1978. *Bee Pollen and Your Health.* New Caanan, CT: Keats.

Wade, Carlson. 1992. *Health From the Hive.* New Caanan, CT: Keats Publ.

Weitgasser, Hans. (no date). Royal Jelly in Dermatological Cosmetics. *Mediziniche Kosmetik.*

Xiao, J. W. 1996. An active peptide inhibiting bacteria in the royal jelly of honey bee. *Acta Entomologica Sinica.* 39:133-140.

Index

Books and Cassettes

#1 *How to Eat Right and Live Longer*—$21.95
  360 pages   6 x 9 inch softbound
Dr. Ingram's most comprehensive book on diet and nutrition. Describes the treatment of a wide range of illnesses through diet and nutritional supplementation. Emphasis is on the nutritional treatment of heart disease, high cholesterol, high triglycerides, diabetes, obesity, allergies, arthritis, neurological disorders, and alcoholism. Step-by-step nutritional protocols, dietary instruction, personalized nutritional/blood analysis, and 100 recipes included.

#2 *Self-Test Nutrition Guide*—$24.95
  336 pages   5 1/2 x 8 1/2 inch hardbound
Test yourself to determine your nutritional deficiencies from *A to zinc*. Other tests show evidence of possible health problems such as adrenal insufficiency, chemical toxicity, thyroid insufficiency, intestinal malabsorption, liver dysfunction, and premature aging. Sugar, caffeine, sulfite, food dye, and MSG overload also evaluated. Each test followed by specific and thorough nutritional recommendations. Find out what you are lacking.

#3 *Who Needs Headaches?*—$13.95
  172 pages   6 x 9 inch softbound
A nutritional approach to solving the migraine dilemma. Emphasizes food allergies, nutritional deficiencies, and hormonal disturbances and how to diagnose them as well as how to reverse them nutritionally. Chapter on structural therapy for tension headaches included.

#4 *Tea Tree Oil: the Natural Antiseptic*—$12.95
  110 pages   5 1/2 x 8 1/2 inch softbound
Some things need to be killed: bacteria, viruses, fungi, parasites, and parasitic insects. Learn how to battle infectious disease with tea tree oil, one of Nature's most versatile and potent antiseptics. Information particularly valuable for homemakers, travelers, wilderness buffs, fishermen, and athletes.

#5 *How to Survive Disasters with Natural Medicines*—$13.95
  137 pages   5 1/2 x 8 1/2 inch softbound
Natural disasters, toxic waste spills, fires, parasite infestations, accidents, radiation leakage, and water contamination all demand immediate action. Learn to deal with both major and minor disasters using only natural remedies which are both safe and effective. Destroy ticks, stop wound infection, end the pain of toothache, neutralize animal/insect bites, abort diarrhea and/or dysentery, treat burns/cuts — all with natural substances.

#6 *Supermarket Remedies for Better Health*—$29.95
  340 pages   5 1/2 x 8 1/2 inch softbound
Reverse health problems with foods, herbs, and spices. Learn to shop for your ailments at the supermarket, health store, and farmer's market. A supermarket juice that reverses heart disease, a vegetable that halts depression, a berry which eliminates stomach aches, a fruit which lowers cholesterol, a berry for poor vision, a protein for great energy, a spice which kills germs and much more. Use supermarket remedies for hundreds of ailments.

#7 *The Cure is in the Cupboard: How to Use Oregano for Better Health*—$19.95
205 pages–Revised Edition 51/2 x 81/2 inch softback
Oregano helps you regain your health and then stay healthy. This is what saved Dr. Ingram's life. Learn how to use oregano and its essential oil for fighting infection and eliminating pain. Combat skin disorders, injuries, wounds, and dental problems. Particularly valuable for fungal infections.

#8 *Lifesaving Cures*—$19.95
320 pages, 6x 9 inch softback
To survive in the 21st century you must know lifesaving cures. This book describes the most powerful remedies for reversing everyday illnesses. With this book of natural cures Dr. Ingram provides hundreds of natural answers for dozens of ailments.

#9 *The Respiratory Solution*—$14.95
157 pages, 5.5x 8.5 inch softback
Learn the most powerful natural cures for reversing dozens of respiratory ailments. Gain fast relief from sinus problems, allergies, mold, bronchial problems, colds, flu and much more using edible natural foods and herbs.

#10 *The Longevity Solution*—$12.95
144 pages, 5.5x 8.5 inch softback
A book that explains the incredible powers of royal jelly. Reverse fatigue, hormonal problems, hot flashes, anxiety, depression, insomnia, irritability, panic attacks, and much more. Stall the aging process with royal jelly.

Cassette Tapes and Programs

#1 *How to Use Oregano for Common Illnesses*—$9.95
A must addition for oregano lovers. Contains detailed information not found in the book. Specific protocols for dozens of illnesses and diseases plus case histories. Learn hundreds of uses for wild oregano oil and herb—from the Doctor himself.

#2 *Professional/Advanced Series*—$89.95*
The Warning Signs of Nutritional Deficiency
4 tapes Total time: 4 hrs Manual: 100 pages, with Judy Kay Gray, M. S.
Master Dr. Ingram's knowledge about nutritional deficiency and natural medicine. Find out how to discern your specific deficiencies; become proficient in spotting nutritional deficiencies in others. Includes lifesaving information on the treatment of disease with nutritional medicine. Become an expert.
* Normal price for this program is $129.95. Save $40.00 when you order from this book.

#3 *Wild Oregano, Lifesaving Spice*—$9.95
Dr. Ingram's famous lecture on the power of wild oregano. Learn all the most compelling facts—why it worked, the research, and true life stories—informative and entertaining.

ORDER FORM

Item	Quantity	Amount
Books		
Book #1 *How to Eat Right and Live Longer*	_____	_____
Book #2 *Self-Test Nutritional Guide*	_____	_____
Book #3 *Who Needs Headaches?*	_____	_____
Book #4 *Killed on Contact: The Tea Tree Oil Story*	_____	_____
Book #5 *How to Survive Disasters with Natural Medicines*	_____	_____
Book #6 *Supermarket Remedies*		
Book #7 *The Cure is in the Cupboard*	_____	_____
Book #8 *Lifesaving Cures*	_____	_____
Book #9 *The Respiratory Solution*	_____	_____
Book #10 *The Longevity Solution*	_____	_____
Cassette Tapes and Programs		
Tape #1 *How to Use Oregano for Common Illnesses*	_____	_____
Tape #2 *Professional Series* (tapes and manual)	_____	_____
Tape #3 *Wild Oregano, Lifesaving Spice*	_____	_____
Sub-Total		_____
Sales Tax (if any)		_____
Shipping*		_____
TOTAL		_____

*Shipping Charges: $5.00 for single books—add $1.00 for each additional book. Cassette tape series add $4.00. Payment by check, money order, or credit card.

Make checks payable to: NAHS P.O. Box 4885 Buffalo Grove, IL 60089
telephone: (800) 243-5242

Use the following for VISA, Mastercard or American Express orders:

Credit Card # _____ Exp. Date _____

Name _____

Address _____

City _____State _____Zip_____

ORDER FORM

Item	Quantity	Amount
Books		
Book #1 *How to Eat Right and Live Longer*	_____	_____
Book #2 *Self-Test Nutritional Guide*	_____	_____
Book #3 *Who Needs Headaches?*	_____	_____
Book #4 *Killed on Contact: The Tea Tree Oil Story*	_____	_____
Book #5 *How to Survive Disasters with Natural Medicines*	_____	_____
Book #6 *Supermarket Remedies*		
Book #7 *The Cure is in the Cupboard*	_____	_____
Book #8 *Lifesaving Cures*	_____	_____
Book #9 *The Respiratory Solution*	_____	_____
Book #10 *The Longevity Solution*	_____	_____
Cassette Tapes and Programs		
Tape #1 *How to Use Oregano for Common Illnesses*	_____	_____
Tape #2 *Professional Series* (tapes and manual)	_____	_____
Tape #3 *Wild Oregano, Lifesaving Spice*	_____	_____
Sub-Total		_____
Sales Tax (if any)		_____
Shipping*		_____
TOTAL		_____

*Shipping Charges: $5.00 for single books—add $1.00 for each additional book. Cassette tape series add $4.00. Payment by check, money order, or credit card.

Make checks payable to: NAHS P.O. Box 4885 Buffalo Grove, IL 60089
telephone: (800) 243-5242

Use the following for VISA, Mastercard or American Express orders:

Credit Card # _____ Exp. Date _____

Name _____

Address _____

City _____ State _____ Zip_____

ORDER FORM

Item	Quantity	Amount
Books		
Book #1 *How to Eat Right and Live Longer*	_____	_____
Book #2 *Self-Test Nutritional Guide*	_____	_____
Book #3 *Who Needs Headaches?*	_____	_____
Book #4 *Killed on Contact: The Tea Tree Oil Story*	_____	_____
Book #5 *How to Survive Disasters with Natural Medicines*	_____	_____
Book #6 *Supermarket Remedies*		
Book #7 *The Cure is in the Cupboard*	_____	_____
Book #8 *Lifesaving Cures*	_____	_____
Book #9 *The Respiratory Solution*	_____	_____
Book #10 *The Longevity Solution*	_____	_____
Cassette Tapes and Programs		
Tape #1 *How to Use Oregano for Common Illnesses*	_____	_____
Tape #2 *Professional Series* (tapes and manual)	_____	_____
Tape #3 *Wild Oregano, Lifesaving Spice*	_____	_____
Sub-Total		_____
Sales Tax (if any)		_____
Shipping*		_____
TOTAL		_____

*Shipping Charges: $5.00 for single books—add $1.00 for each additional book. Cassette tape series add $4.00. Payment by check, money order, or credit card.

Make checks payable to: NAHS P.O. Box 4885 Buffalo Grove, IL 60089
telephone: (800) 243-5242

Use the following for VISA, Mastercard or American Express orders:

Credit Card # _____ Exp. Date _____

Name _____

Address _____

City _____ State _____ Zip_____

NOTES